The Livewire Guide to Going, Being and Staying Veggie!

Juliet Gellatley

First published by Livewire Books
A member of the Namara Group
34 Great Sutton Street, London EC1V 0DX

Reprinted 1998

British Library Cataloguing in Publication Data
A catalogue record for this book is available from the British Library.

IS13N 0 7043 4939 6

Typeset in Bembo 12pt/14pt by Intype Ltd
Printed and bound in Great Britain by
Cox & Wyman Ltd, Reading, Berkshire

This book to be returned on or before the last date below.

Juliet Gellatley went vegetarian at 15 years old and has spent most of her life fighting for animals. After her degree in zoology and psychology she became the Vegetarian Society's first Youth Education Officer and rose to be its Director. On the way, she launched Britain's first-ever youth campaign against factory farming, increasing the number of schools offering veggie meals from 13 per cent to 65 per cent and launched *Greenscene*, Britain's only magazine for young vegetarians. In October 1994 she launched *Viva!*, an exciting new vegetarian and vegan charity for adults and young people.

To Tony for your unwavering faith in me,
your encouragement, support, boundless talent and,
most of all, love.

To all the young people who fight to save the
animals and create a more compassionate world.

And to all animals. There is a growing awareness
that all life is precious and interdependent.
One day you will be free.

Contents

Introduction

It all starts here . . . with the ultimate guide to going, being and staying veggie.

This book will take you through the change from being a meatie to a vegetarian – every step of the way. Every question answered, every doubt knocked on the head and every concern sorted.

If you're already veggie, this book will give you the confidence and knowledge to argue for your beliefs. If your parents are worried, it will put their minds at rest. If you're short of facts, you'll find them here.

Farming has become a secret industry where animals are crammed together behind closed doors, away from prying eyes. Section 1 of this book shines a spotlight into the darkest corners and reveals what it's really like. As you'll discover, even the animals you see in the fields are not the examples of contentment you're led to believe – they, too, often have sad and secret lives.

Around the world, more and more people are giving up meat and fish as they find out its real cost – and it's not the price that's charged in the supermarket! Section 2 looks at the real cost of meat: the effect farm animals have on the environment; the way that fishing is destroying our oceans; and how the poor of the world starve so farm animals can eat. It's no wonder that over half a million young people in Britain alone are veggie.

Despite this, the old myths about eating meat survive. We need meat, some people say. Meat is healthy! We're meant to eat meat! I've scoured the world for proof of these statements and guess what? It isn't there. What I did find was a mass of scientific and medical proof that vegetarians are healthier and live longer. Section 3 sorts out the fantasy from the facts, the reality from the rubbish.

Giving up meat and fish used to be seen as a bit of a weirdo thing to do but now it's supported by scientists and doctors everywhere. All the same, going, being and staying veggie means having the courage to stick by what you believe. Section 4 helps you stand up for yourself – at school, at home and with your friends. It even gives you all the info and support you need to campaign to save animals.

How do I know all this? Because I've been through it! I became veggie when I was 15. Since then, I've spent most of my working life trying to save animals, talking to tens of thousands of young people and campaigning all over Britain. The most important thing I've learnt is that one person can make a difference.

Throughout their life, one person eats 5 cows, 20 pigs, 29 sheep, 760 chickens, 46 turkeys, 15 ducks, 7 rabbits, one and a half geese and half a ton of fish.

What better reasons are there for going, being and staying veggie?

Section 1
Animal Farm

Introduction

I want to ask you a question. Do you think that animals can feel things like pain or fear, or know what it means to be too hot or too cold? Unless you're a complete drongo who's just arrived from Mars, the answer's got to be yes, hasn't it?

Well, actually, you're wrong! According to the European Union, the organisation that makes up a lot of the rules about how animals in Britain should be treated, farm animals are exactly the same as a CD player or a Frisbee. In their view, animals are nothing more than products — and nobody worries too much if you ill treat a Frisbee. The reasons go back a long way.

During the Second World War there was a shortage of food in Britain and Europe, so to make sure people got enough to survive, food was rationed. When the war ended in 1945, farmers in Britain and elsewhere were asked to grow as much as they could so there would never again be such shortages and hardships. There were almost no rules or regulations, farmers just got on and did it. In an effort to grow as many crops as possible, they used masses of fertiliser on the land and loads of pesticides to kill weeds and insects. To produce as much meat as possible, they also started cramming animals together in sheds. There were so many that there wasn't enough land to graze them all on.

Even with pesticides and fertilisers, farmers couldn't grow enough grass and hay to feed all their animals with so they started to introduce new foods such as wheat, corn and barley, most of it imported from other countries. They also added chemicals to the feed to control diseases because so many animals in one place provided a perfect breeding ground for bugs.

Once animals were kept in sheds rather than roaming free, it was easy for farmers to pick out the ones that grew fastest or had the most meat on them and breed only for them. This is called selective breeding and it was repeated year after year. The animals were also given food 'concentrates' that made them grow even faster – often dried, ground-up fish and bits of other animals. Sometimes it was even pieces of their own kind – chickens fed back to chickens, bits of cows fed to cows. It was all done on the basis of 'waste not, want not'.

As the years went by new ways were found of making animals grow faster and bigger, because the bigger and faster they grew, the more money could be made from selling their meat. All the time they were treated less like animals and more like Frisbees. Instead of individual farmers working the land to make a living, food production became big business. Many farmers turned into mega-big producers and City companies invested large amounts of money in them. Of course they wanted something back – more money. So farming became an industry where profits were much more important than how the animals were treated. It's what's now known as agribusiness, and, in Europe, Britain led the way.

The bigger and more powerful meat producers became, the less the government tried to control them. Large amounts of money were involved and this was spent on equipment, machinery and automation to take the place of farm workers. And that's how Britain's farming got where it is today – a massive industry which employs fewer farm workers per acre than any other country in the world.

Before the Second World War, meat was a bit of a luxury, something people ate once a week or on special occasions. Now, producers grow so many animals that meat is something most people eat every day in one form or another – bacon, sausages, burgers, ham sandwiches, pepperoni pizza, chicken nuggets – it's even in some biscuits, cakes and pastries as animal fat. It's *everywhere*! But what about the animals themselves, the 760 million or so which are killed for meat in Britain every year? This section looks at what happens to the animals that become the meat products in our lives.

Chapter 1
Piggy on a Plate

'We use everything but the "oink"' boast producers when they talk about pigs. Every single thing about pigs has been worked out to the last dot and comma, like ticking off a checklist of things to do: 'How can I get them to: 1) produce as many piglets as possible; 2) use as little energy as possible; 3) eat as little food as possible; 4) put on as much weight as possible; 5) cost me as little money as possible?'

Producers have asked and answered every question in the world about raising pigs except one: 'What about the animals?' Anyone who had asked that question would never have come up with the 'dry sow stall'.

There are roughly 800,000 breeding sows (female pigs) in the UK and, as I write, over half of them are being kept in metal-barred stalls so narrow that the bars or concrete walls almost touch their sides. They can take half a pace forward, half a pace back and can just about lie down with difficulty. Some are tethered to the floor with a big, broad collar around their necks or their middles just to make sure that they don't leap out. Pigs that don't move, use up less energy, so more of the food they eat turns to meat.

There's no bedding in these stalls either, because that costs money and would have to be changed regularly. Instead, the pigs stand on concrete or wooden slats which their droppings are supposed to fall through. Some does, some doesn't and when the sow lies down there is usually something pretty nasty for her to lie in.

And don't believe the old tale about pigs liking muck and filth – they don't. In the wild, pigs roll in mud but believe it or not, that works in much the same way as facial mud packs. They certainly don't like standing on slats because their feet aren't made for it and they often end up with really bad back and leg pains.

I've walked through pig sheds and seen these conditions for myself. It nearly blew my mind that so much cruelty could happen under one roof. Animals which naturally live together in family groups, which are bright and intelligent and as inquisitive as dogs are chained in solitary confinement. They're with hundreds of other pigs but can barely see them, can't touch them and can't do anything but eat the same boring dry pellets in the container in front of them – all day, every day.

The reason these sow stalls are called 'dry' has

nothing to do with the weather either. It just means that for the 16½ weeks they're there, the sows are not producing milk. In fact they're pregnant. When it comes nearer the time for them to give birth, they're moved to things called farrowing crates.

These poor sows are treated just like breeding machines. They're forced to churn out five litters of piglets every two years, with as many as 12 or 13 piglets in a litter. Wild pigs breed only once a year and produce nothing like this number of piglets. And unlike wild pigs, the factory-farmed sows never get the chance to be a real mother.

In the farrowing crate, a metal implement a bit like a huge comb with big gaps between the teeth separates the sow from her piglets. She lies on her side and the bars stop her from nuzzling her young, from licking them or doing any of the things she would like to do. The piglets can get to their mother's teats to suckle but no other contact is possible.

The reason for this contraption? To stop the mother from rolling on her young, say the producers. This can sometimes happen in the first few days after birth when the little piglets are too slow to get out of their mother's way. The reason is that farm pigs have been bred to be unnaturally big and fat and do sometimes flop around. But the few producers who allow their sows a more natural life without the farrowing crate still manage okay. Producers say that using this device shows how much they care for their animals. It's really about caring for their bank balance because a lost piglet is lost profit.

After three or four weeks of suckling, the piglets are

taken away from their mothers and put into piggiboxes, which are stacked one on top of another. In the wild they would suckle for at least another two months. I have watched piglets which have been allowed a more humane life in the open air scamper around, chasing each other, tumbling and playing and generally being full of mischief, much like puppies. These factory-farmed piglets are crammed together so they can't even escape from each other, let alone play. Out of frustration and boredom they often start to bite each other's tails, sometimes causing terrible wounds.

So how do the farmers stop it? Easy – they cut off the piglets' tails or take their teeth out. It's cheaper than giving them more space.

Pigs can live for 20 years or more but these piglets don't last longer than five or six months, depending on whether they are killed for pork or pork products such as pork pies and sausages, ham or bacon. For a few weeks before they die they are taken from the boxes and put into fattening pens, still crammed together, still with no bedding and still with absolutely nothing to do. In the USA, 'Bacon Bins' were developed in the 1960s – here, piglets are kept alone in bare cages so small they can hardly move. This stops the piglets 'wasting' energy on exercise, so that they get fat quicker.

For the mother, life of a sort goes on. As soon as the piglets are taken from her, she is strapped down and a boar (the male pig) is allowed to make her pregnant again. Left on her own she would be naturally choosy about her mate, just like most animals, but here she has no choice. Afterwards, it's back to the dry sow stall for another four months of total boredom while the next litter grows inside her.

If you ever get the chance to see sow stalls, you'll notice that some of the pigs gnaw at the bars in front of them. They do it in a particular way, repeating the same movements over and over again. Animals in zoos sometimes do something similar, such as pacing backwards and forwards in a set way. It's known to be a result of extreme stress and has been likened in a report on the welfare of pigs by the government-supported body, CRB Research, to a nervous breakdown in humans.

For sows who aren't imprisoned in sow stalls, life isn't much happier. They are usually crammed together and still have to produce just as many piglets in the farrowing crate. Only a tiny proportion of pigs are allowed to live in the open air — what's called free range.

Yet wild pigs once lived in Britain, in the woods that covered over half the country, until they were hunted to extinction in 1525. They were reintroduced in 1850, but were wiped out again by 1905. These pigs foraged in the wild for food like nuts, roots and worms, and they lived with other pigs. They sheltered under the cool of the trees in summer and built huge nests of sticks and dried grass to keep them warm in winter.

A pregnant sow would also build a nest, often a metre high, for her litter and she would travel miles to find the materials to make it. Watch a pig in a farrowing crate and you will often see her searching the tiny space for . . . something. It's the old habit of wanting to build a nest. And what is she given? Not a stick, not a strand of straw – nothing.

Luckily, the dry sow stall is illegal in Britain from 1998 and, although most pigs will still live in overcrowded conditions, it is a step forward. But 40 per cent of all meat eaten in the world comes from pigs. They are consumed more often than any other animal and are factory farmed in every corner of the globe. Also a huge amount of ham and bacon eaten in Britain comes from other countries, such as Denmark, where even more pigs are being put into sow stalls. The biggest step forward for all pigs is for people to stop eating them! It's the one thing which will have an immediate effect. No more pigs will be put through this torment just for you.

'If young people realised what was involved in the factory farming of pigs they would never touch meat again.'
James Cromwell, Farmer Hoggett in the film *Babe*

Chapter 2
Fowl Play

How do you think chickens live? I'm talking here about the ones reared for meat rather than the ones that lay eggs, because there is a difference. In farm yards, scratching around in the straw? Wandering around fields having dust baths? Afraid not! Today's 'broilers' (an American word meaning to 'grill', as in cook) are crammed 20,000 to 100,000 or more in one shed and never see so much as a ray of sunlight.

Imagine a huge shed with wood shavings or chopped-up straw on the floor and not a window anywhere. When the day-old chicks are first put in, there seems to be plenty of room, with the little balls of fluff running around everywhere, eating and drinking from the automatic troughs. The bright lights stay on the whole time, apart from half-an-hour in every 24 when they are turned off. This isn't so the chicks can have a nap. It's because if they never see darkness and the lights go out accidentally because of a power cut, they panic and some might be crushed to death.

Seven weeks later, just before they're killed for meat, these little chicks have been tricked into growing at twice the speed they would naturally. The constant light is part of the trick, making them eat much longer and much more than they would normally. So is the food they're given. It is unnaturally 'high in protein', making them put on weight — and it often contains ground up bits of other chickens.

Think of the same shed now, with the chickens fully grown. Each bird weighs an amazing 1.8 kilogram and has only as much space as a computer screen. You can hardly see the straw and wood shaving, which is just as well because it hasn't been changed since the first day and is now soaked with seven-weeks'-worth of droppings. The chickens have grown so fast that they still 'tweet' like baby birds and their eyes are still blue like babies but their size is the same as an adult bird.

If you look carefully you'll see that some birds are dead. Others are not bothering to eat or drink but just sit and pant. This is because their hearts can't pump enough blood to feed their huge bodies. The dead and dying are collected and disposed of every day. According to the farmer's magazine, *Poultry World*, around 12 per cent of all chickens die like this — 72 million every year — before they even reach the slaughterer's knife. And the number is increasing all the time.

There are also things that you *can't* see. You can't see that their food always contains an antibiotic medicine which these chickens need every day to ward off the

13

diseases which would spread like wildfire in such over-crowded conditions. You can't see that four out of five have broken bones or deformed feet and legs because their bones aren't strong enough to carry their huge weight. And you can't see that many of them have burns and blisters on their legs, feet and breasts.

These are ulcers caused by the ammonia in their droppings. It is unnatural for any animal to spend its life standing on its own droppings, and ulcers are just one of the results. Ever had little ulcers on your tongue? Painful, aren't they? Well these poor birds are often covered in them.

In 1994, 676 million chickens were killed in Britain, and almost all of them lived in these awful conditions because we're told, people want cheap meat. It is a similar story in the other European Union countries. In the USA, six billion broilers are killed each year, 98 per cent of which are factory farmed in the same conditions that I've talked about here. But when were you or your folks last asked if you wanted chicken meat that cost less than tomatoes and involved such cruelty? Unfortunately, scientists are still looking for ways to make them put on weight even faster so they can kill them sooner. The faster they grow, the worse for the chickens but the more money the producers make.

It isn't just chickens either that spend their whole lives in overcrowded sheds, it's the same for turkeys, and for ducks for that matter. If anything, it's even worse for turkeys because they've still got many of their natural wild instincts, so their captivity is even more stressful.

I bet you think a turkey is a waddling white thing that looks like an extra from the Hammer House of Horrors. Well, a turkey is really a very handsome bird, with black wing and tail feathers that shine red-green and copper, and a white bar across their wings.

Turkeys still live wild in some parts of the USA and South America. They roost in trees and nest on the ground but you have to be very quick to catch one, as they can fly at up to 88 kilometres an hour and can keep this speed up for over a kilometre-and-a-half. Turkeys wander far and wide looking for seeds, nuts, grasses and small crawly things to eat. The great fat creatures produced for our tables, that can't fly and can barely walk, have been created by producers determined to make them bigger and meatier.

Not all baby turkeys (or poults as they're called) are reared like chickens in the completely artificial environment of broiler sheds. Some are put in pole barns, which do have natural light and ventilation. But even in pole barns the growing poults have almost no space and the floor still becomes a soaking mess.

It's much the same story for turkeys as it is with broiler chickens – the growing birds suffer ammonia burns and constant doses of antibiotics, as well as heart attacks and pain because their legs can't support their huge weight. The crowded conditions lead to stress and boredom, and as a result the turkeys peck each other. Producers have developed a way of stopping the birds from harming each other in this way – they slice the end of their beaks off with a red-hot blade when they're just a few days old. In the wild or when there's

15

enough space around them, turkeys don't peck each other in this way.

Some of the most pitiful turkeys are the ones kept for breeding. They can grow to the huge weight of six stone and have such diseased hip joints that they can barely walk.

Doesn't it seem strange that when people sit down for Christmas dinner, to celebrate peace and forgiveness and all the better things in life, they do it by first cutting something's throat and killing it? When they 'ooh' and 'aah' and say what a lovely turkey they're munching into, they close their eyes to the pain and filth that was its life. And when they carve its huge breast they probably don't even know that this great lump of flesh has turned turkeys into freaks. We have produced a creature that can't even mate without us doing it for them using artificial insemination. Not a very merry Christmas for them!

Chapter 3
Assault and Battery

A fourteen-year-old friend of mine became a vegetarian and gave up eggs. Nothing unusual in that, you might say. No, except that her father owned one of the biggest battery-egg plants in Europe. Her Saturday morning job was to go around all the cages and take out the dead birds! She knew firsthand what egg production is all about.

Forget all those pictures of clucking hens sitting contentedly on their eggs or being followed by a trail of tweeting little chicks. The birds that produce 90 per cent of eggs in Britain (and the rest of the EU, the USA and other industrialised nations) have been turned into laying machines. They never see a cockerel (male bird) so the 300 eggs they lay every year are not fertile and could never hatch even if they were given a chance to sit on them, which they're not.

Let me take you through the life of a battery hen. A day after being hatched in big, industrial sheds, the chicks are divided by sex; males on the left-hand conveyor, females on the right. The conveyor carries the male chicks away to a bin in which they are dumped.

These chickens have been specially bred to produce eggs and to survive on the smallest possible amount of food, so they're very scrawny. Because of this, male chicks are no good for meat, no good for laying eggs, in fact they're good for nothing, so the factory gasses them – 40 million every year. Or sometimes they are crushed to death – it just depends on the fancy of the particular factory.

The females are taken to cages, where they stay until they're about four months old and able to lay eggs. It's then that they are put into wire battery cages, five chickens together in a space about 45 centimetres by 50 centimetres, not much bigger than a microwave oven.

Now for a quick bit of maths. If the cage is 50 centimetres wide and a chicken's wings are 76 centimetres wide when they're spread out, what does it mean? It means that not even one chicken has enough space to spread her wings properly, so with five to a cage they have absolutely no chance.

In a single shed there can be thousands of cages holding tens of thousands of birds – row upon row stacked four or five deep with nothing between them but wire mesh. (In battery farming 20,000 hens per shed is considered quite a small number.) The droppings from the birds in the top tier of cages fall on to the birds in the cages below, before finishing up on the ground. If you're ever unlucky enough to go into a battery shed, be prepared for the stink, because they're usually not cleaned out for between 18 months and two years – the length of the birds' life. After this time the chickens' egg-laying begins to slow down so they are killed to make way for new birds, even though they might live naturally for another five years or more. They finish up as stock cubes or in pies or baby food – or even in school meals!

If ever you get the chance, watch a farmyard chicken as it goes about its day. It struts and wanders, scratches the ground for tasty bits to eat, pushing aside the grass and earth with powerful thrusts of its feet. It hardly ever stops moving, wandering far and wide across fields. Also watch it when it wants to lay an egg. It goes somewhere quiet, secluded and safe and away from humans and even other chickens.

Hens make such good mothers that the word used to describe them – broody – is used to describe human mothers. When the hen's chicks hatch, she watches over them with an eagle eye. Wherever she goes her chicks follow and at the first sign of danger she gives a special 'cluck' and they all dive for safety beneath her wings. When the day is hot and the mother hen rests, her chicks will sometimes climb all over her and doze off on her broad, feathered back. The perfect sun bed!

These are the same creatures that we cram into tiny cages where they can do none of these things. Everything about their lives is automated – the feed, the water and the egg collection. Battery-hen cages all have sloping floors so that the eggs they lay immediately roll down on to a conveyor belt and away from the hen.

Watching a hen lay an egg in this cage is a very sad sight. It can take up to an hour and she will pathetically try to hide from the other chickens, scrambling beneath them attempting to disappear from view. Farmers will tell you that because the hens lay eggs it shows they're happy. This is like saying that everyone who goes to the loo is happy; they are both bodily functions which we can't control.

It's not really surprising, then, that battery chickens get frustrated, bored and angry, and that this can make them aggressive. They will often take it out on their cage mates by pecking them; so their beaks are sliced off when they're chicks in order to stop what producers call their 'vice'. People used to think that beaks were like fingernails: bits of dead material with no feeling. But research by scientists at the Institute of Animal Physiology in Edinburgh has shown that they are extremely sensitive and contain lots of nerve endings. When their beak is cut off, some chicks die from shock, and some from bleeding, and it's possible they feel the amputation throughout their lives. But battery hens are subjected to other hardships as well.

A combination of little fresh air and no daylight, overcrowded conditions and selective breeding has led to a whole host of diseases in the battery sheds. Things like egg peritonitis, Gumboro disease, prolapses, leukaemia, and infectious bronchitis, all end up meaning the same thing – distress, suffering and death for two million chickens every year.

One of the most common ailments amongst battery hens is brittle bone disease which results in their bones snapping like dry twigs. Chickens evolved from jungle fowl, which in the wild lay only about 12 eggs a year. Battery hens lay about 300 a year and the calcium which should build their bones is used to make egg-shells. The result is weak and brittle bones that break easily. According to the British government's own research council, a third of all battery hens have broken bones. What must it be like to spend your life like that, especially in a crowded cage being pushed and shoved all the time?

That, then, is the life of a battery hen. The University of Edinburgh looked at all the scientific studies and concluded that 'battery hens suffer' and that the cages should be outlawed. Anyone who says they're wrong should be locked in a telephone box for a month with four other people, and then asked again!

Today, most eggs come from battery hens. Don't be conned by the words 'country fresh', 'farm fresh' or 'fresh from the countryside' either. Unless it says 'Free range' on the box, the eggs you're buying are from battery hens. Unfortunately, free-range eggs aren't always all their cracked up to be, either. The rules on free range allow producers to keep 1,000 birds per hectare of land, but if they are to move about as they choose, to stretch their wings and legs, run, peck, scratch, find bugs, beetles and seeds, and do all the things that hens like to do, 250 would be much better. Some of the big producers cram thousands of hens into a shed, stick a few little openings in it and call it free range. Many of the chickens never even go outside because they're afraid of crossing other birds' territory or because they don't feel safe surrounded by so many other hens.

For most free-range hens, life isn't any better than for the turkeys which are kept for meat in the pole barns. The majority of sheds are just like these, over-crowded, smelly and dirty. Whatever the system, all the male chicks are still killed at only a day old.

Chapter 4
Counting Sheep

Competition, we're always being told, is good. It's what gives us choice and variety and it's what keeps prices down. But where sheep are concerned, all competition has done is make their lives sadder and more painful.

Sheep always look so content grazing away in the countryside, their little lambs running and jumping around, full of the joys of spring. Don't be fooled. That's about all the joy there is because in Britain alone four million lambs don't even survive the first few days of life. In Australia, the sheep capital of the world with 135 million animals, it's considered 'normal' for 20 to 40 per cent of lambs to die within this time. It's usually the cold or starvation that kills them.

In Britain and the West, most people don't eat sheep meat – called mutton – they eat lamb. The natural time for ewes (female sheep) to give birth to their lambs is in the spring but competition between farmers has meant they're now trying to get the sheep to give birth earlier, at the end or even middle of winter. If farmers can be amongst the first to sell 'new season's lamb' they get more money for it.

Over many thousands of years, wild ewes have evolved to ovulate (become fertile) and mate in autumn so their lambs are born when the worst of the winter has passed and the grass has started to grow. It's exactly the same with farmed sheep. But many farmers now treat the ewe with hormones which trick her body into thinking it's autumn while it's still summer. By mating their sheep much earlier, farmers are causing lambs to be born in the middle of the very worst winter weather.

Sheep which live on low-lying land, in ordinary fields in Britain usually give birth to their lambs in sheds. The lambs are turned out into the fields soon after birth, whatever the weather. The farmers also give their ewes fertility drugs to make them produce two or even three lambs when they would naturally only produce one. This causes problems because a sheep has only two teats (or nipples). The 'spare' lambs are immediately taken away from the mother and sent to market.

Bewildered, frightened and denied the tender care of their mothers, these newborn lambs await their future shivering in the cold. Prodded and poked by farmers to see how fat they are, they are bought for just a few pounds each. Some are bought by fancy restaurant owners — but if you can understand how someone can look at these bleating, scared creatures and see them as 'Today's special – baby lamb roast with garlic and rosemary,' please tell me.

What farmers are working towards is to make sheep bear three litters every two years. To do this they have to distort the ewes' natural instincts by controlling them with hormone treatments. This is the start of factory farming for sheep and before long you may not see so many of them in the fields. Their home will be one big, overcrowded, disgusting shed.

Sheep which live on higher ground, like the Pennine hills or the Welsh mountains, live a much wilder, more natural life. They aren't manipulated in the same way, but competition means that things are changing here as well. Farmers are cramming more and more sheep on to the hills, where there never was much grazing for animals in the first place. To save money, they're cutting down on the number of shepherds employed to watch over them, and cutting out the extra feed that they used to provide through the winter. Because fatty meat isn't popular any more, farmers are also trying to get rid of the layer of fat just below the sheep's skin through selective breeding. But this is, along with extra food, what helps the sheep keep warm when the icy winds of winter howl.

Although more and more sheep are dying because of interference like this, farmers are breeding larger and larger numbers, and there are now nearly 45 million sheep in Britain alone. Unfortunately, their future is not a happy one.

'I visited my parents to help with lambing and I helped deliver a baby lamb. It was beautiful. The next day a farmer brought us a leg of lamb and somehow it seemed all wrong. I couldn't reconcile what I'd been doing all day — bringing life into the world, just to heartlessly take it. I became a vegetarian. '

Jakki Brambles, first woman to host a daytime daily programme on BBC Radio 1

Chapter 5
Moo to You

How do we get milk? Don't just say 'from cows'! Would it surprise you to learn that the only reason we get cow's milk is because the cow has had a calf – just as the only reason a woman produces milk is because she's had a baby? The big difference is that we don't take the baby away from the woman and use her milk in our tea. But that's what we do to dairy cows and we do it every year for as long as they live.

Wouldn't it be nice, though, if a cow produced enough milk to feed her calf and still had enough left over for us to drink and make into cheese, yoghurt, ice cream, butter and all the other things we make from milk? Guess what – she does! The poor dairy cow has been so selectively bred over the years that she now gives ten times as much milk as her calf could ever drink. But we still take the calf away after only

24 hours so we can have it all – up to 10,000 litres of it from each cow every year.

Once you've seen a mother cow staring after her newborn little calf in panic as it's led away to a shed, never to be seen by her again; once you have heard her bellows of grief at its loss, it's very hard to look at the dairy industry in the same way. But this is only the start of the story for dairy cows, which are probably the hardest working, most abused of all farm animals. The reason they don't get much sympathy is because their problems aren't easy to see – in fact dairy cows appear quite happy. It all seems so nice and peaceful as they quietly munch away at the grass or lie in the sunshine chewing the cud. (They bring their food back up and chew it again which is one reason why they can digest grass and we can't.) But next time you're near a field of them – they're usually the black and white ones called Friesians – take a closer look.

Look at their udders. These milk-producing organs are far bigger than they ever are in wild cows. If you watch you'll see how they often affect the way the cows walk, the size forcing their legs apart. This unnatural way of walking causes damage to the feet, making many cows limp. Their foot problems are made worse by the hard concrete floors of the sheds in which they're kept over winter. Cows' hooves aren't designed to stand on concrete for months on end.

As a result, cows suffer from a disease called laminitis – an inflamation of the membranes on the inside of the hoof. Does it hurt? Professor John Webster, head of the animal husbandry department at Bristol University, isn't in any doubt. He says that studying the feet of slaughtered cows shows that nearly 100 per cent of them have this crippling disease. He says 'To understand the pain of laminitis caused by foot damage it helps to imagine crushing all your fingernails in the door then standing on your fingertips.' For cows with extreme laminitis there is no cure and they are destroyed.

But dairy cows have other problems too. If you look at their rear ends, you'll see that their bones stick through the skin. It often looks like a piece of thin material that's been thrown over a coat hanger. This is because a dairy cow is either giving milk, carrying a calf or doing both things at the same time. Not only does she produce a massive quantity of milk for nine months after the birth of her calf, but for most of that time she is pregnant with her next calf, and has to provide nourishment for the new calf inside her. Her only break is during the last three months of her pregnancy when the farmer stops milking her so that all her strength can go to help build her growing calf. Because a dairy cow gives birth every year, this punishing routine never stops.

Wild cows produce only enough milk for their calf – about one-tenth the amount produced by dairy cows – and as a result they have tiny udders. Nor do they become pregnant while they're still feeding their calf, as this would rob them of nearly all their energy and jeopardise their survival. In contrast, a dairy cow uses up so much energy she is usually badly nourished, hungry and exhausted. The cow's huge output of milk puts an unnatural strain on her udders and in about one-third of cows, these become inflamed and infected. This painful disease is called mastitis and results in thick pus oozing out of the cow's teats.

After giving birth just two or three times, the tissues in a dairy cow's body starts to break down from overwork and poor nutrition. This is why dairy cows are killed when they're between four and seven years old, even though they could live to be 20 or more. It's like a girl being completely physically worn out while she's still a teenager.

None of this happens to the cows used to breed beef cattle. They're not milked for humans and so produce just the right amount of milk for their calves. Like wild cows, they have tiny udders, not the huge things you see on dairy cows, which means their bodies can absorb all the nutrients they need.

You might expect producers would look at exhausted dairy cows and say it was time to give them a rest. No chance! Dairy corporations are experimenting with a hormone called BST (bovine somatotropin) which will make cows give even *more* milk – as much as 40 per cent more. Through selective breeding, they're producing new types of cow which will give *twice* as much milk again. It seems you just can't satisfy greed!

And what happens to the worn-out dairy cows? They're sent to the slaughterhouse and killed for 'low grade' meat products like hamburgers, pies, stock cubes and, again, school dinners!

Humans are the only species on the planet that drink another animal's milk, so what happens to the calves? Not one of the one million or so calves born to dairy cows in Britain each year ever see their mothers again after the first day or two. About 330,000 female calves are kept to replace their worn-out mothers who are killed. Some of the heftier looking calves are kept and allowed to grow into beef cattle. But the majority, about 450,000 every year, are sent to market at just a few days old, before they can even eat solid food or drink without sucking from a teat. They're destined to become veal calves.

In Britain, these animals are usually bought by special dealers who send them abroad to France, Holland and Denmark. The calves are crammed together in big lorries and when they reach their new homes, it's not green fields they find but a darkened wooden box with slats to stand on – a crate so small they can't even lie down properly or turn round. No bedding, no companionship, just darkness and torment.

The whole purpose of this crate system is to keep the calves as cheaply as possible. It's also designed to make them anaemic – lacking in iron – so their flesh will stay baby-white. This means they never see daylight and never chew grass or hay (as they would naturally do) because both these things would turn their flesh from white to pink, the colour it is meant to be. Instead, the calves are given a non-stop diet of milk and water with no solid nourishment of any kind. The animals will lick their crates or swallow their own hair, so desperate are they for something satisfying. Offer them your fingers and they will suck them greedily, as much for comfort as anything else.

After 22 weeks of this misery, the calves are taken from their crates and killed. For what? White veal for the 'gourmet's' dinner table in posh restaurants. Even though the crates are illegal in Britain, it's perfectly okay to send the calves abroad and then import their meat – which just shows how people can side-step the law to their own advantage.

Campaigning groups all over Europe have lobbied to extend the ban on veal crates from the UK to include all EU countries. Agricultural ministers from the European Union have accepted recommendations to phase out crates in the year 2008. This is a positive step but even once the crates are abolished, calves will still be separated from their mums at one day old. They will still be kept anaemic and will never feel the sun or be able to graze; and they will still only have a tiny $1.2m^2$ space in which to stand – and may still not be given any bedding. The only real difference is that at a few weeks old they will be moved from being kept alone into a crammed pen with other calves.

So what about the calves that are kept for beef? In Britain, like almost everywhere else in the world, beef comes from castrated male cattle called bullocks or steers. Some beef cattle come from dairy cows and these herds grow up together, often being allowed to graze on open fields. Increasingly, however, these calves are moved into crowded sheds when they're about a year old, and fed a high-protein diet to make them grow more quickly.

In the USA, few beef cattle are ever seen wandering around as they do in the movies because they're mostly crammed together in feed lots – big, open-air pens. Americans, followed closely by Australians, eat more beef than any other nation and 100,000 cattle are slaughtered every 24 hours. So much beef is consumed in the USA that there isn't enough land to graze all the cattle on which is why they're penned up. It's easier to bring the food and water to them and there can be hundreds, often thousands of cattle, in each pen. It's just another kind of factory farming.

The steer have very little space to move around in, and stand in their own mess for a year or more, living on high-protein food that makes them put on weight quickly. Once again, the animals are fed high levels of antibiotics and other chemicals to ward off the diseases caused by overcrowding. This system of beef production was introduced in Britain in 1987.

There are other ways of growing beef cattle and the kindest method is by using 'suckler' herds. Calves are allowed to stay with their mothers until they're about two years old, and before they start eating grass they can suckle as much milk as they want. Animals in these herds are able to interact as they would in the wild and to some extent behave in the way that herds of cattle do naturally. Well, until the young bullocks are taken away and killed that is!

A huge beast as heavy and powerful as a cow could cause real havoc to humans if it wanted to, but it doesn't. Instead, it pays a terrible price for being so docile. We take its young away from it and literally milk it dry. Producers have turned the cow into a milk or meat machine – which is strange, as we don't need either.

'Eating veal is inexcusable.'
Gaby Roslin, TV presenter

33

Chapter 6
The Road to Misery

Animals are not usually killed on the farms where they're kept, so they have to be moved to slaughter-houses, called abattoirs. As slaughterhouses get bigger and fewer in number, animals are transported longer and longer distances before being killed. As a result, hundreds of millions of animals are trucked around Europe each year. Unfortunately, some are transported even further afield, to different countries in North Africa and the Middle East.

So why are animals exported? The answer is simple – money. Most of the sheep that go to France and Spain and other EU countries are not killed immediately, but are allowed to graze for a week or two first. So they can recover from the journey? Because people feel sorry for them? No – so that the dealers can claim they are Spanish or French sheep, label them 'Home Produced' and sell the meat at a higher price.

The laws which govern how farm animals are treated differ in every country. For example, some have no laws about the way animals are killed while others, like Britain for example, have slaughter regulations. Under British law, animals must be made unconscious before they're killed. Frequently this doesn't happen or the regulations are simply ignored. However, the situation is no better and may even be worse in other European countries where there are virtually no controls. In Greece, animals may be beaten to death with hammers, in Spain sheep often have their spinal column severed with a screwdriver, and in France animals' throats are cut while they are still fully conscious.

You'd think that if the British were really serious about protecting animals we wouldn't allow them to go to countries where there are no abattoir controls or where the controls are poorer than in Britain. Not a bit of it. It's perfectly okay for farmers to export live animals to any country they choose, to be killed in ways which are forbidden in their country of origin.

In 1994 alone, about two million sheep and 450,000 calves were exported from Britain for slaughter. About 70,000 pigs were also exported. However, pigs often die en route – generally from heart attacks caused by fear, panic and stress. Not surprisingly, all animals find being transported stressful, whatever the distance travelled.

Just try and imagine what it must be like to be an animal which has never known anything but the pen in which you have been kept or the fields in which you graze. Suddenly, you're prodded and poked into a lorry and driven for hours on end. Often you are separated from your own herd and forced together with animals you don't know – unnatural behaviour for most animals, and very distressing.

The conditions in the lorries are often disgusting too. Most of the lorries used have metal trailers of two or three tiers. The urine and droppings from the animals at the top fall on those below. There is no water, no food, no bedding, just a metal floor and tiny gaps in the sides for ventilation.

When the lorry doors slam shut behind them, animals are on the road to misery. They may travel for 50 hours or more, be starved, driven crazy with thirst, be beaten, kicked, punched, dragged by their tails or ears or prodded with electric goads. Animal welfare organisations have tracked many lorry loads of animals and in almost every case, they found that the recommended journey times were exceeded and the recommendations about rest periods, feeding and watering were ignored. There have also been numerous news reports of whole lorry loads of sheep and lambs being left in the baking sun without water until as many as a third of them died from thirst and heat stroke.

Animals are crammed together, bounced around and frequently in pain. According to the RSPCA (Royal Society for the Prevention of Cruelty to Animals), more than two-thirds of all sheep and lambs are bruised, some badly, by the time they get to the abbattoir, and up to one million chickens are injured every year as a result of their heads or legs becoming caught in the transport crates. I have seen sheep and calves

36

so crowded together that their legs stuck out of the ventilators in the sides of lorries, obviously causing great distress. Independent organisations say that animals are sometimes crushed to death.

For those animals exported abroad, this nightmare journey may also include being transported by plane or shipped by ferry or boat, sometimes on rough seas. Conditions here can be particularly bad with lack of ventilation leading to overheating and death from heat stroke or lack of water.

It's certainly no secret how exported animals are treated. Many people have witnessed it and some have even shot videos as proof. But you don't have to search out ill-treatment with hidden cameras; it's everywhere for everyone to see.

I have watched sheep being punched in the face with full force because they were too frightened to jump down from a lorry. I have seen pigs kicked and stamped on as they were forced to leap from the upper tier of a truck to the ground two meters below, just because the unloaders were too lazy to put up a ramp. And I have seen them break their legs on landing and then watched as they were dragged and kicked into the slaughterhouse. I have witnessed boars having their snouts broken with an iron bar because the fear and overcrowding had made them bite each other. 'It stops them thinking about fighting,' said the man who did it.

But perhaps the most horrible sight I have ever seen was in a film made by the organisation Compassion in World Farming, which showed what happened to a young, fully-grown bull that had broken his pelvis on the transport ship and was unable to stand. The handlers applied an electric cattle prod to its testicles and delivered a 70,000 volt shock to try and force it to stand. When humans do this to other humans it is called torture and the world condemns it.

I made myself watch as for 30 minutes the men continued to shock the crippled beast and each time they did, it bellowed in pain and scrambled at the deck, trying to stand. Eventually, they shackled a chain to the bull's leg and hauled it up with a crane, dumping him on the quayside. An argument between the ship's captain and the harbour master followed and eventually, the bull was hoisted back up and dumped on the deck of the ship, still alive but barely conscious. As soon as the ship left the harbour the poor creature was dumped in the sea to drown.

British courts say it is quite legal to send animals to face this kind of abuse and claim that there are regulations in all European countries governing how animals are transported. They claim that European inspectors check on their treatment. But what is written on paper and what happens in reality are very different things. The truth is that the people who are supposed to do the checking admit that they have never carried out a single check throughout the whole of Europe. A European commissioner confirmed this in answer to a question in the European parliament.

In 1995, many people in the UK were so disgusted by the trade in live exports that they took to the streets. They protested at British ports and airports such as Shoreham, Brightlingsea, Dover and Coventry, where animals were being shipped or flown to other countries. They even tried to stop the lorries loaded with calves, sheep and lambs from reaching the ports and airports by direct action. Despite the fact that public opinion was in support of the protestors, the British government refused to ban the trade.

Instead, it announced with a big fanfare that the European Union had agreed regulations which would, for the first time, control the journey times of animals in Europe. In fact, all that had been done was to give official approval to what was already happening. For example, the journey time for sheep was set so that they could still be transported without a break for 28 hours – the time needed to truck them from northern Europe to southern Europe. There were no proposals to improve inspections so even if transporters continued to break the new regulations, there'd be no one to check on them.

But the fight against live exports hasn't ended there. Some protesters have decided to continue the struggle by challenging the British government in the courts, including the European Court. Others have continued to protest at the ports and airports, as well as at the farms where the animals are bred. Still more have tried to make the world aware of the plight of exported animals.

As a result of these efforts, it is likely that live exports from Britain to Europe will one day be stopped. Ironically, a scandal about a deadly disease called BSE (or mad cow disease) stopped the export of calves from the UK in 1996. The British government had finally admitted that people were at risk from eating beef infected with BSE which was widespread amongst British herds, so not surprisingly, other countries refused to buy British cattle (for more on BSE, see pp. 94–96). It is unlikely, though, that the trade between European countries will end altogether in the foreseeable future. Pigs will still be sent from Holland all the way to southern Italy, and calves will be sent from Italy to veal crates in Holland. Their meat will still be sold in Britain and around the world. This trade in misery lies at the heart of eating meat.

Chapter 7
Murder, She Wrote

Animals don't run happily into a slaughterhouse, throw themselves on their backs, shout, 'Here you are, have a chop!', and then die. There's a sad truth that every carnivore has to face: If you eat meat then animals will be killed for you. How death is dished out depends upon the animal.

Most of the animals killed for meat are chickens – 676 million of them each year in the UK alone. They're taken from the broiler sheds to the 'processing plants' – a much nicer expression than slaughterhouse! It's all timed like clockwork with lorries arriving at set times throughout the day. The chickens are taken from the lorries and shackled upside down to a conveyor system by their feet. It's exactly the same for turkeys and ducks.

There is something really strange about these

chicken processing plants – they are so clinical and soulless. They are always brightly lit and, apart from around the actual slaughter point, fairly clean, if a bit wet and sloshy. They are also very mechanical and very automated. People walk around in white overalls and hats saying good morning to each other. It's almost as if they're making televisions or canning peas.

The give-away is the slowly-moving line of fluttering white birds, which never seems to stop. In fact this conveyor belt often keeps going day and night. The first thing the strung-up chickens meet is an electrified, water-filled bath. They are dragged across it by the conveyor so their heads dangle in the water. The electricity is supposed to stun them so they're unconscious by the time they reach the next stage – the throat cutting.

Sometimes this cutting is done by a blood-stained human with a knife. Sometimes it's done by a blood-stained automatic cutting machine. As the conveyor belt moves on, the chickens are supposed to bleed to death before being dunked into what's called the scalding tank – very hot water that loosens their feathers.

Well, that's the theory. The reality is often horribly different. At the stunning bath, some chickens raise their head and miss it so they are fully conscious when their throats are cut. When the cutting is done by a machine, which is more often the case, the blade is set at a particular height. But not all chickens are the same size, which means the shorter birds get cut on the head and the longer ones on the breast. Even if they are cut in the neck, most automatic machines sever the back or side of the neck and rarely cut the carotid arteries. Either way, it's not enough to kill them, only to wound them very badly. Millions of birds reach the scalding tank alive and are literally boiled to death.

Dr Henry Carter, past President of the Royal College of Veterinary Surgeons, says in a 1993 report on the slaughter of chickens:

> procedures in far too many poultry slaughterhouses do not ensure that the birds are adequately stunned, leaving an unknown number alive and still conscious when they enter the scalding tank. It is high time that politicians and legislators put an end to practices that are unacceptable and inhumane.

The slaughterhouses where the bigger animals such as lambs, sheep, pigs and cows are killed, are very different. They too are becoming more mechanised like a factory but, automated or not, they are one of the most horrible things I have ever seen. Most slaughterhouses are big, echoey places with huge shackles and dead animals hanging from the ceiling. The noise of clanking metal mixes with the sound of frightened animals squealing, bellowing or bleating. There is the sound of men laughing and joking with each other. They are all interrupted by the 'crack' of the special pistols. There is water and blood everywhere and if death has a smell, this is it – a mixture of shit which the frightened animals produce in quantity, dirt, opened guts, and fear.

All the animals brought here die from the same cause – loss of blood after having their throats cut.

However in Britain, they are all supposed to be made unconscious first. Two different methods are mainly used for this – electrical stunning and the captive bolt pistol. This is how they're supposed to work.

To stun an animal into unconsciousness, electric tongs – like a big pair of scissors with headphones instead of blades – are clamped on to its head by the slaughterer. These are held there for a few seconds and an electric shock applied. The unconscious animals – usually pigs, sheep, lambs or calves – are then hoisted up in the air by a chain attached to one back leg. Then their throats are cut. It's called 'sticking' and the animals are meant to die without regaining consciousness.

The captive bolt pistol is usually used on larger animals, like adult cattle. The pistol is placed against the animal's forehead and fired. A metal bolt about 10cm long flies out of the barrel, shatters the animal's forehead and enters the brain, making it unconscious. To make sure, a 'pithing rod' is pushed through the hole and the brains are stirred. The cow or steer is then hauled up and its throat is slit.

What really happens is often very different. The animals are unloaded from the lorries into a series of pens called the lairage. One at a time, or in groups, they are taken to the stunning point. When electric tongs are used, the animals are often stunned in front of each other. Don't let anyone tell you that animals don't sense what is going to happen to them: just watch pigs getting more and more agitated and panicky as their turn gets closer. Their squealing is enough to tear you up.

Because the slaughtermen are paid by how many animals they kill, they try to work as quickly as possible and frequently don't keep the tongs in place for longer than a second or two. With lambs they often don't bother to use them at all. The animals which are stunned might collapse from the shock and even be paralysed but they are often still conscious when they are stuck. I have actually seen pigs hanging upside down with their throats cut, wriggle free of the chains, drop to the ground covered in blood and try to run away.

Cattle are forced into a special stunning pen before the captive bolt pistol is used on them. Done properly, they are made unconscious immediately, but it isn't always like that. Sometimes the slaughterer hits the wrong spot and the cow is in agony while he prepares the pistol and has a second shot. Sometimes the cow jerks away and again the shot might miss. Sometimes, with old equipment, the bolt from the pistol doesn't break through the cow's skull. All these botched shots cause mental and physical agony to the animal.

One survey, carried out by the RSPCA, found that 7 per cent of animals weren't stunned properly. With strong, active young bulls, it was a staggering 53 per cent. In a video which was shot secretly inside an abattoir, I witnessed one poor steer being shot eight times before he collapsed. I also saw much else that made me feel sick: uncaring, brutal treatment of defenceless animals carried out not as an occasional mistake but as the normal way of working. I saw pigs' tails being broken as they were rushed to the stunning point; lambs being slaughtered without any stunning at all; an old, frightened and panicking pig being ridden around the slaughterhouse like a rodeo horse by a callous young slaughterman.

For religious slaughter, sometimes called ritual slaughter, different rules apply. For Jews it is called 'Shechita' and for Muslims 'Halal', but in both cases the animals are not stunned before being stuck, and it can take up to six minutes for them to lose consciousness as they bleed to death.

The methods of ritual slaughter are laid down in Jewish and Islamic teachings which date back thousands of years. For Halal slaughter there are strict rules about the knife being sharp and not having any nicks or blemishes on the cutting edge. This was introduced out of concern for the animals to ensure they were killed as efficiently as possible and not hacked to death. In addition, the animals are killed one by one, so as to prevent them from panicking.

The animals are killed while still conscious because an unconscious animal might have been diseased and there were no ways of checking its health. In both religions, the blood is considered unclean and it was believed that a conscious animal would pump out its own blood more efficiently from its dying body. In fact studies have shown that it makes no difference if the animal is conscious or unconscious, and some Muslim slaughterhouses do stun before slaughter.

Many Jews and Muslims are opposed to the whole process of slaughter, ritual or otherwise, and have become vegetarian because of it. So have a lot of other people!

Special Bonus Facts

The number of animals killed for meat in Britain in one year was:

Chickens	676 million
Pigs	15 million
Cattle	3 million
Sheep	19 million
Turkeys	38 million
Ducks	11 million
Geese	1 million
Rabbits	5 million*
Deer	10,000*

(Figures taken from the UK government's Ministry of Agriculture, Fisheries and Food Slaughter Statistics for 1994, except * which are estimates. The population of Britain is 56 million.)

'I wouldn't want to kill an animal and I don't want to have them killed on my behalf. By not being involved with their death I feel I have a happy secret alliance with the world and I sleep much more peacefully because of it.'

Joanna Lumley, actress

Chapter 8
Munching Monsters

The taste for killing living creatures and then eating them seems to have no limits. You would think the hundreds of millions of animals killed every year in Britain would be enough butchery and carnage for anyone, but some people are never satisfied and are always looking for a different experience – something new on their table to eat.

As every year goes by, more and more exotic animals are appearing on restaurant menus. Already it's ostriches, emu, quail, alligators, kangaroo, guinea fowl, bison, deer – even guinea pigs. Soon it will be anything that can walk, crawl, jump or fly. One by one, we are taking animals from the wild and imprisoning them. Creatures like the ostrich, that live in family groups and run free over miles of African plain, are crammed into tiny, muddy fields or sheds in the chill of Britain.

From the moment it's decided that it's okay to eat a particular animal, a process of change begins. Eventually everything about that animal's life is altered — how it lives, where it lives, what it eats, how it reproduces, how it dies. And every time a change is made, it is for the worse.

The end product of human interference is usually a poor pathetic creature whose natural instincts we've tried hard to erase. We alter animals so badly that in the end, they often can't even breed unless we do it for them. And the ability of scientists to change animals is growing more powerful every day. With the most recent technique of all, genetic engineering, there are almost no limits to what we can do.

Genetic engineering involves altering the biological plan that makes every animal, humans too, exactly what they are. It may seem strange when you look at a human body to think that it is following a plan but it is. Every freckle, every mole, the height, colour of the eyes and hair, the number of fingers and toes, are all part of a very detailed scheme. (I suppose it makes sense, really. When a team of builders arrives on a piece of land to put up a sky-scraper they don't say, 'Right, you start in that corner, I'll start here and we'll see what happens!' They have a whole set of plans in which everything has been worked out to the last screw and nail.)

And in a way, that's how it is with all animals. Except that there isn't just one plan or blueprint for each animal, but millions of them. Animals (including humans) are made up of hundreds of thousands of millions of cells and at the heart of every cell is a nucleus. Packed in every nucleus is a molecule called DNA (deoxyribonucleic acid) which contains genes. These hold the plan for building that particular body. In theory it is possible to grow an entire animal from just one of its cells – something so small you can't even see it without a microscope.

As you probably know, every baby begins as a cell which is created when a sperm fertilises an egg. This cell is a mixture of genes, half from the man's sperm and half from the woman's egg. It multiplies and grows like wildfire and the genes are responsible for what the baby eventually looks like – the shape and size of its body, even the speed at which it grows.

Again, in theory, it's possible to mix the genes of one animal with the genes of another, producing something which is half and half. Already in 1984, scientists at the Institute of Animal Physiology in the UK were able to produce a 'geep' – a cross between a goat and a sheep. What is more usual however, is to take tiny sections of the DNA, or a single gene, from one animal or plant and add it to another animal or plant. This is done at the very start of life, while the animal is still little more than a fertilised egg. As it grows, the new gene becomes part of that animal and slightly alters it in some way.

This process of genetic engineering has become very big business indeed. Huge multinational companies are spending billions of pounds on research, mostly to develop new foods. The first of these 'genetically modified products' are now beginning to appear in the shops all over the world. In 1996, approval was given in Britain for shops to sell tomato puree, rapeseed oil and yeast for bread making, all of which had been altered using genetic engineering. Nor do shops – in Britain at least – have to tell you which products have been genetically altered. So you could, in theory, buy a ready-made pizza which included all three of these foodstuffs and you'd never know. They also don't have to tell you if any animals have been made to suffer for what you are about to eat. And in the genetic research into producing meat some animals have suffered, believe me.

One of the first known genetic engineering disasters was a poor creature in America called the Beltsville pig. It was meant to be a meaty super pig and, to make it grow bigger and faster, scientists introduced a human growth gene into the DNA of an ordinary pig. What they produced was a big pig which was in constant pain.

The Beltsville pig had joints so diseased with chronic arthritis that when it tried to walk, it could only crawl on its knees. It couldn't stand up and most of the time it lay still, suffering from a whole range of other diseases. This obvious experimental disaster was the pig that scientists allowed the public to see – there were other pigs from the same experiment which were in such a disgusting state that they were kept locked behind closed doors.

But the lesson of the Beltsville pig hasn't stopped the experimenting. In fact, genetic scientists have now produced a supermouse, double the size of an ordinary mouse. This mouse was created by introducing a human gene into the supermouse's DNA that causes cancers to grow extremely fast. Scientists are now trying the same gene out in pigs but because people wouldn't want to eat meat that had a cancer gene in it, they've renamed it a 'growth gene'.

In the case of the Belgium Blue cow, genetic engineers identified the gene responsible for increasing the cow's muscle size and doubled it, thereby ensuring bigger, meatier calves. There was also, unfortunately, a downside. The female cows born as a result of this tinkering have slimmer hips and a narrower pelvis than normal – the very part of the body a calf has to pass through during birth.

It's not too difficult to work out what happens. A bigger calf and a narrower birth passage means that it is often extremely painful for the mother to deliver her calf. Mostly, the genetically altered cows are unable to give birth at all. The solution is to cut them open (in what's called a caesarian section) and remove the calves. This operation may be carried out every year, sometimes for each delivery and each time the cow is cut open, the more painful it becomes. In the end the knife is cutting not through normal flesh but thick scar tissue, which takes longer and longer to heal. We know that when women have multiple caesarian births (something that luckily doesn't happen too often) the operation is excruciatingly painful. It's the same for the cow. Even scientists and vets agree that the Belgian Blue cow must suffer great pain – but the process goes on just the same.

An even weirder bit of tinkering has been done to Swiss Brown cows. It was discovered that these cows had a genetic weakness which meant they often developed a particular brain disease. But oddly, when this disease flared up, the cows gave more milk. When scientists located the gene that caused this disease they didn't use the knowledge to cure it – they made sure the cows *got* the disease just so they would give more milk. Scary, or what?

In Israel, scientists have found the gene in chickens that is responsible for featherless necks as well as the one responsible for curly feathers. Using the two genes together they have created a bird that is almost bald. The few feathers it does have are curly, exposing the bare flesh beneath. The reason? So producers can factory farm chickens in the heat of the Negev desert where temperatures reach a blistering 45°C.

So what other little treats are in store? Some of the projects I've heard about include research into producing hairless pigs; experiments with creating wingless battery chickens so more can be crammed into each cage, as well as work aimed at producing sexless cattle, and vegetables with fish genes.

Scientists insist that it is safe to alter nature in this way. But a big animal, like a pig, contains millions of genes; and scientists have mapped just a hundred of these at most. When a gene is changed or a gene from another animal is introduced, they have no idea how the other genes are going to react – they can only guess. And no one can say what the long-term consequences may be. (It's a bit like the builders on our imaginary building site changing a steel beam for a wooden one because it looks prettier. It might hold the building up – but on the other hand, it might not!)

Other concerned scientists have made some pretty worrying forecasts about what this new science might bring. Some say that genetic engineering could produce a whole new range of diseases for which our bodies have no resistance. Where genetic engineering has been used to change insects, some scientists are worried that it might result in new, uncontrollable pests.

The multinational companies responsible for introducing and encouraging this research offer all kinds of reason why genetic experiments must go on. They say that it will result in fresher, tastier, different and maybe even cheaper food. Some even claim it will be possible to feed the world's starving people. This is just an excuse. A comprehensive report from the World Health Organisation in 1995 made it clear that there's enough food to feed everyone on the planet already; and that other economic and political reasons are preventing it from reaching those in need. There is no evidence to show that the money invested in genetic engineering will be used for anything other than to make a profit.

The long-term results of genetic engineering may be a disaster but there's one thing we already know – animals are already suffering in the race to produce more and more meat as quickly and cheaply as possible.

Section 2
Saving the World

Introduction

Some people say eating meat or not eating meat is a personal thing. They say it's everyone's right to choose and they wouldn't dream of telling anyone they should give up meat. I'm not one of these people and I'll tell you why. Let me paint a picture for you.

If someone offered you a cake and told you how much sugar was in it, how many calories, what it tasted like and how much it cost, you might decide to eat it. That would be your choice. If, after you'd eaten it, you had to be taken to hospital and the person said, 'By the way, it's also got arsenic in it!', you'd probably feel well choked.

Choice is useless unless you're told all the facts that affect that choice. When it comes to meat and fish we're told almost nothing and most people are pretty ignorant of the facts. Who would believe you if you told them that children in Africa and Asia go hungry so we in the West can eat meat? What effect do you think it would have if people really knew that a third of the world's surface is turning to desert because of meat production? How shocked would they be to know that over one half of the world's oceans are on the point of environmental collapse because of fishing? Or what about the deadly food poisoning which comes from meat?

These are the hidden doses of arsenic in the meat and fish eater's cake. These are the realities of being a carnivore. That's why I'm not a quiet vegetarian — it's much too important for that.

Chapter 9
Food for a Future

Here's a conundrum for you: What food is it that the more we produce, the more people starve to death? Give up? The answer's meat!

Most people find that hard to believe, but it's true. The reason is that meat is an incredibly wasteful way of producing food and on average, just to produce 1 kilogram of it, 10 kilograms of vegetable protein is used. That vegetable protein could be fed directly to people instead.

The reason this leads to starvation is because people in the wealthy West use so many of the world's crops to feed their farm animals. It's even worse than that too; because the West has so much power it can insist that some less wealthy countries grow food for the West's animals when they could be growing it for their own people.

So what is the 'West' and who are these wealthy people? The West is that part of the world which controls most of the money, most industry and has the best standard of living. It's made up of the European countries, including Britain, and the USA and Canada, so it is sometimes referred to as 'North'. Although there are some wealthy countries in the 'South' such as Japan, Australia and New Zealand, most countries in the southern half of the world are comparatively poor.

About 5600 billion people share this planet, roughly one third of them in the rich North and two-thirds in the poorer South. In order to live, we all use the planet's crops and natural products – but we don't all use the same amounts. For example, a child born in the USA will, throughout its life, use 12 times as many resources as a child born in Bangladesh: 12 times more wood, copper, iron, water, land, and so on.

Some of the reasons for these differences in wealth lie back in history. Hundreds of years ago armies from the North conquered countries in the South and turned them into colonies – in effect, they now owned them. They did it because these countries were rich in all kinds of natural resources, including food.

The European colonists used the countries they invaded to supply the products they needed for their industries. Many people who lived in the colonies had their land taken from them or had to grow crops for their European colonisers. During this period, millions of people in Africa were also captured and taken back to Europe and America to work as slaves.

This was one reason why the North became so rich and powerful.

Colonialism ended forty or fifty years ago after the colonies won their independence, often by fighting for it. Although countries such as Kenya and Nigeria, India and Malaysia, Ghana and Pakistan are now supposed to be independent, colonisation has left them poor and dependent upon the North. And that's how it still is in many countries. So, when the North says it wants grain for its cattle, the Southern countries don't have much choice but to grow it. It's one of the few ways they can get money to pay for the technology and industrialised goods they need, things they can only buy from the North.

It isn't just products and money that the North has more of. It also has an unfair share of the world's food. Take Bangladesh and the USA again: the average food intake for a Bangladeshi is 1930 calories per day, while for an American it is 3650 calories. It has been estimated that the minimum amount of food needed for good health is 2360 calories per day. So you can see, the average person in Bangladesh has too little food while the average American eats too much. And about one-third of the average American diet is meat.

Of course it isn't just Americans who eat large amounts of meat, it's all the populations in the wealthy North. In Britain, the average amount of meat eaten per person is 71 kilograms per year. In India, on the other hand, the average is only 2 kilograms of meat per person. The average American eats 112 kilograms of meat every year, a lot of which is beef. In the United States, children between the ages of 7 and 13 eat nearly six-and-a-half hamburgers each week; and fast food restaurants alone sell 6.7 billion hamburgers every year.

This enormous appetite for hamburgers has an effect on the whole world. It's only in this century and particularly since the war that people have started to eat meat in such a big way – and now meat-eaters are literally devouring the earth. Believe it or not, there are three times as many farm animals in the world as there are people – 16.8 billion of them. Animals have huge appetites and can munch their way through mountains of food. But most of what goes in one end comes out the other end and is wasted. All animals farmed for meat eat more protein than they produce – even the most efficient. Pigs eat nine kilograms of vegetable protein to produce one kilogram of meat, while chickens eat about five kilograms for one kilogram of meat. The remaining kilograms are mainly lost as manure.

Animals in the United States alone eat enough wheat and soya beans to feed 1900 million people – about one-third of all the people in the world, or the whole population of India and China put together. But there are so many cows that even that's not enough and to keep these non-stop munching machines going, yet more cattle food is imported from abroad. The USA even buys beef from the poor countries of Central and South America, and all these cattle have to be fed in a similar way.

Perhaps the worst example of waste is in Haiti, officially one of the poorest countries in the world where most people have to survive on 1900 calories per day. Much of the country's best agricultural land is used to grow a kind of grass called alfalfa and big international companies fly their cattle to Haiti from the USA so they can graze on the alfalfa and put on weight. The animals are then killed and the carcasses are flown back to the USA to provide even more burger meat.

To make way for this American cattle, the ordinary people of Haiti are pushed back on to the mountain slopes, where they must farm on the poorest land. To grow enough food here to survive, they overuse the land until it becomes poor and useless, and eventually just blows away in the wind. It's a vicious circle which sees the people of Haiti get poorer and poorer.

But it isn't just American cattle which are consuming all the world's food. The European Union (EU) is the single largest importer of animal feeds in the world – and 60 per cent of this comes from countries in the South. Try and imagine how much space would be taken up if you lumped together the whole of Britain, France, Italy and New Zealand. That's the amount of land taken up in the poorer countries of the world to grow food for Europe's animals. And that's on top of all the fields already in use in Europe for grazing and growing animal feed crops.

Grazing and feeding the 16.8 billion animals farmed for meat is using up more and more of the world's agricultural land. What's even more frightening is that the amount of land for growing food is dwindling rapidly while every year the number of people being born is growing. The two sums just don't add up.

As a result, the poorest two-thirds of the planet are

sliding deeper and deeper into a life of starvation and poverty in order to support the wealthiest one-third. In 1995, the World Health Organisation issued a strongly-worded report called *Bridging the Gaps* which described the situation as a global catastrophe. According to this report, hundreds of millions of people in the South spend their whole lives in extreme poverty, and about 11 million children die every year from diseases caused by starvation. The gap between North and South is growing wider and if things don't change, famine, poverty and disease will spread even more rapidly throughout two-thirds of the world.

The tremendous waste of food and land used for producing meat is at the heart of this problem. According to Sir Crispin Tickell of Oxford University, a UK Government adviser on environmental issues, it is logistically impossible to feed the world's population of 5.6 billion people on a meat-based diet. There just aren't enough resources. Only 2.5 billion people – less than half the world's total – could be fed on a diet in which 35 per cent of the calories people consumed came from meat. (The very diet now eaten in the USA.)

Just imagine how much land could be saved and how many people could be fed if all the vegetable protein wasted on animals was fed directly to people instead. And before you say; 'But I don't eat grass!' I'm not just talking about grass. Nearly 40 per cent of the world's wheat and corn is fed to animals and huge amounts of land are given over to growing things such as alfalfa, peanuts, turnips and tapioca to be used as animal food. This land could just as easily be used to grow food for people.

If the whole world ate a vegetarian diet – that's plant foods and dairy products such as milk, cheese and butter – Tickell states there would be enough food right now to feed 6 billion people well. In fact, if everyone became vegan and cut out all dairy products and eggs, the world's population could be fed on less than one quarter of the land that's used at present!

Of course eating meat isn't the only cause of world hunger but it *is* one of the most important. So, never let anyone tell you that veggies care only about animals.

'My son persuaded myself and my wife, Caroline, to become vegetarians by pointing out that if the world ate the grain instead of feeding it to farm animals, no one would starve.'

Tony Benn, MP

Special Bonus Fact

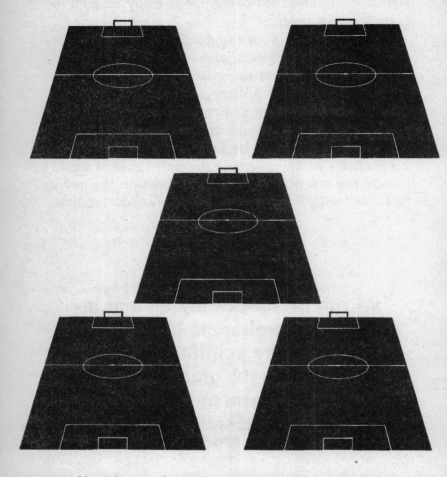

An area of land the size of 5 football pitches (10 hectares) will grow enough:

meat to feed **2** people

OR...
maize to feed **10** people

OR...
grain to feed **24** people

OR...
soya to feed **61** people

Chapter 10
Planet on a Plate

The world is so old that it can be hard to get your head around just how long it's been here. There is the sky and all the creatures which inhabit it; the oceans and their teeming mass of different life forms; the animals and plants which crowd the surface, as well as the ones which burrow and crawl beneath it. We are talking wonder!

One way of getting a handle on the timescale of 'when' and 'how' and 'which' is to reduce the whole of the world's life to just one year – nearly 5 billion years telescoped down to one. On this reckoning it is now one minute to midnight on 31 December and the world began almost exactly 12 months ago on 1 January.

Using this one year timescale, a few days after the world was born, bacteria came into existence. But it wasn't until ten months later, in October, that sponges inhabited the seas. At the start of November, jellyfish began to float around and spiders started to spin their webs. On 25 November there were fish for the first time in the water and ferns waved their fronds on the land. Dinosaurs began their rule over the world on 1 December and fifteen days later they disappeared.

Just a quarter-of-an-hour ago, at 15 minutes to midnight, humans came into being. The Industrial Revolution started only two seconds ago, and in that tiny flicker of time, people have caused more damage to the world and the things which live on it than in the whole of the rest of its life. And things are getting worse. For most of the time we have been on the planet – about five million years if you count our early human ancestors – we have been vegetarians. We only started hunting about 1.5 million years ago. In the words of *Guardian* newspaper journalist Colin Spencer, that's the equivalent in individual terms of an 80-year-old having been a vegetarian until the age of 65.

At first sight, there may not seem to be much connection between meat eating and the huge environmental problems facing the world, such as global warming, spreading deserts, disappearing rain forests, and acid rain. In fact, meat production is at the heart of these and many other global disasters.

The truth is, the world is fast running out of the land needed to feed meat animals. It isn't just that one-third of the world's surface is turning to desert but also the fact that the best agricultural land has been farmed so intensively, that it is starting to lose its fertility and won't grow as many crops. Once, farmers used to 'rotate' their fields, growing a different crop each year for three years and during the fourth year growing nothing. They called it leaving the fields 'fallow'. This method ensured that different nutrients were absorbed by different crops each year and it allowed the soil to recover its fertility.

As the demand for animal feed grew in the years following World War Two, the rotation system began to disappear. Now, farmers often grow the same crops year after year in the same soil. The only way they can do this is to saturate the land with artificial fertilisers and control the weeds and insects with pesticides. Eventually, the structure of the soil begins to break down and it becomes thin and lifeless and easily eroded. A half of all the agricultural land in Britain is now at risk from being washed away by rain or blown away by the wind.

On top of this, enough of Britain's hedgerows have been torn up to encircle the earth three times. The forests that once covered most of the British Isles have been cut down and less than 2 per cent remain. Over 90 per cent of British ponds, lakes and marsh lands have been drained – all to make bigger fields to grow more crops to feed more animals. The story is much the same all over the world.

Modern fertilisers are nitrogen based and unfortunately not all of the fertiliser used by farmers stays in the soil. Some is washed into streams, rivers and ponds where the nitrogen can cause poisonous 'blooms'. This occurs when the algae that grows naturally in the water starts feeding on the excess nitrogen. Because it's been fertilised, the algae quickly grows out of control, shut-

71

ting out all sunlight from the other plants and animals. These blooms can use up all the oxygen in the water, choking plants and animals alike to death.

Nitrogen also gets into human drinking water. In recent years, it has been linked with cancer and to a disease called blue-baby syndrome which destroys the oxygen-carrying red blood cells in newborn babies, and which can kill them. The British Medical Association reckons that 5 million Britons regularly drink water that contains too much nitrogen.

Pesticides are also a problem. These poisons spread slowly but surely through the food chain, becoming more and more concentrated all the time, and once in the body they tend to stay there. Imagine this: From a field, pesticides are washed by rainfall into a nearby pond and some of the chemicals are absorbed from the water by weeds. Little shrimps eat the weeds and day after day the poison builds up inside them. Then a fish eats lots of the poisoned shrimps and the poison becomes even more concentrated. Finally, a bird eats lots of these fish and the poison gets stronger still. So, what started off as a weak solution of pesticide in the pond water can build up through the food chain until it is 80,000 times stronger than its original concentration, according to the British Medical Association.

It's the same story with farm animals that eat crops which have been sprayed with pesticides. The poison concentrates in the animals' tissue and then becomes even stronger in the people who eat these animals. In fact most people nowadays carry pesticide residues in their bodies. However, the problem is worse for meat eaters because the levels of pesticide found in meat are about 12 times stronger than the levels found in fruit and vegetables. The *UK Pesticides Monitoring Journal* accepts that 'foods of animal origin are the major source of pesticide residues in the diet.'

No one is yet sure what effect these concentrated pesticides have on us but many doctors, including those of the British Medical Association, are extremely worried. They fear that the increasing levels of pesticides stored in people's bodies may lead to cancers and to a reduction in the body's ability to fight off disease. The Institute of Comparative Environmental Toxicology in New York reckons that throughout the world over one million people suffer from pesticide poisoning every year and 20,000 of them die.

Tests on UK beef have shown that two in seven samples contained a chemical called dieldrin at levels above the EU limits. Dieldrin is rated as 'extremely hazardous' by the World Health Organisation which believes it can cause birth defects and cancer. The American government admits that dairy products followed by beef are the main source of the highly poisonous organochlorine pesticides now found in humans.

There are other environmental problems, as well. Because so many farm animals in Europe and the USA are kept in sheds, there is now so much manure that no one knows what to do with it all. There is too much to put on the land and it's too poisonous to pour into the rivers. It is called 'slurry' (a nice-sounding name for liquid shit) and stored in ponds called (believe it or not) 'lagoons'.

In Germany and Holland alone, there are three tons

of this stored 'slurry' for every member of the population – that's getting close to 200 million tons of the stuff! Through a complicated series of chemical reactions, acid evaporates from the slurry causing acid rain. In some parts of Europe, slurry is the single biggest cause of acid rain causing enormous environmental destruction – killing trees, making rivers and lakes lifeless, and damaging the soil. Large parts of Germany's Black Forest are dying, in Sweden some rivers are almost completely dead, and in the Pel region of Holland, 90 per cent of all the trees have died because of acid rain from pig poo.

When you look outside Europe, the environmental damage caused by animals farmed for meat is even greater. One of the biggest problems is the cutting down of rain forests to create grazing land for beef cattle. Wild forests are turned into cattle pastures and their meat is sold to Europe and the USA for hamburgers and steak. It's happening wherever rain forests exist but the main countries involved are in Central and South America. We're not talking a tree here and a tree there, but an area the size of Belgium chopped down every year. Since 1950, half of all the world's rainforests have been destroyed.

This is one of the most short-sighted policies imaginable because a rainforest's soil is extremely thin and lifeless and needs the protection of its canopy of trees. It has a very short life as pasture. After six or seven years of grazing cattle, the soil won't even support grass any longer, and turns to dust.

Now you might ask, what good is a rainforest to anyone anyway? Well, these forests are home to half of all the creatures and plants on the planet. They are nature in perfect balance, soaking up water from the rains and recycling every leaf and fallen branch as food. As they grow, the trees absorb carbon dioxide from the air and replace it with oxygen, acting like the planet's lungs. These magnificent wildernesses provide almost 50 per cent of our medicine and all kinds of discoveries are still being made of new animals and plants.

It seems a crazy way to treat one of the world's most valuable resources but some people, the landowners, become extremely rich on it. The timber and meat they sell provides big profits and when the land becomes lifeless, they simply move on, chop down more trees and get richer. The tribal people who live in the forest are forced off their land and sometimes even killed. Many finish up in shanty towns where they have almost no means of surviving.

The rain forests are destroyed by a technique called slash and burn. This means that the best trees are chopped down and sold, while the rest is slashed to the ground, piled up and burnt. And this contributes to yet another problem – global warming.

When the sun warms the planet, some of that warmth is held against the earth's surface by the gases which make up the world's atmosphere. (It's a bit like wearing a coat in winter to keep warm.) Without that heat, our planet would be a cold and desolate place. So some warming is a good thing. But too much and everything starts to go haywire. This is what's called global warming and it happens because some of the gases created by humans float up into the atmosphere and trap even more heat against the earth's surface.

One of these gases is carbon dioxide (CO_2), and one way of producing it is to burn wood. The slashing and burning of rain forests in South America creates fires so big it's hard to imagine. When astronauts first went into space and looked down at Earth, there was only one artificial structure they could see with their naked eyes – the Great Wall of China. But in the 1980s they saw something else made by humans – great drifting clouds of smoke from the burning Amazon jungle.

As the rainforests burn to make way for cattle ranching, all the CO_2 stored by the trees and shrubs, sometimes over hundreds of years, is released and floats upwards to add to global warming. According to the governments around the world, this process alone causes one fifth of the total global warming of the planet.

Once the forests are cleared and the cattle starts grazing, the problem becomes even worse. Because of their digestive processes, cows fart and belch an awful lot. When they do they release methane, a gas which is 25 times more effective at trapping heat then CO_2.

If you think a little fart here or there isn't a problem, think again. There are 1.3 billion cows on the planet and every one of them produces at least 60 litres of methane every day. Between them, this amounts to 100 million tons of methane every year. That is not a little fart! Even the fertilisers sprayed on the land add to global warming by producing nitrous oxide – a gas which is a staggering 270 times more effective at trapping heat than CO_2.

No one really knows what the result of all this warming might be. What we do know is that the earth's temperature is slowly rising, and as it does so the polar ice caps are beginning to melt. In Antarctica, temperatures have risen by an average of 2.5°C over the last 50 years and 8000 square kilometres of ice shelf have disappeared. In just 50 days in 1995, 1300 square kilometres of ice vanished.

As the ice melts and the oceans of the world become warmer, they will expand and rise. There are many predictions about how much the sea will rise, from one metre to five metres, but most scientists now believe it's inevitable that there will be some rise. It means that many islands around the world such as the Seychelles and Maldives will disappear and large areas of low-lying land and even whole cities such as Bangkok will be flooded. Even large parts of Egypt and Bangladesh will disappear beneath the water.

Britain and Ireland won't escape either, according to the University of Ulster. There are 25 places at risk of flooding, including Dublin, Aberdeen and the coastlines of Essex, North Kent and large parts of Lincolnshire. Even London isn't considered totally safe. Millions of people will be forced to flee from their homes and their land – but to where? There is already a shortage of land!

Perhaps the biggest question of all is what will happen at the top and bottom of the world? There are huge areas of frozen land at the north and south poles called 'tundras' and they present a very worrying problem. Frozen in their soils are millions of tons of methane gas and as the tundras warm, the methane gas will be released. The more that's released, the greater the global warming and the warmer the tundras get – and so on and so on. It's called 'positive feedback' and is believed to be unstoppable once it starts. No one has yet predicted what the result will be but it's unlikely to be good.

Unfortunately, that's not the end of meat as a global destroyer.

Believe it or not, the Sahara desert was once green and lush and grew wheat for the Romans. That has all gone now and the desert is spreading, growing 320 kilometres in some places in just 20 years. The main reason for this is overgrazing by goats, sheep, camels and cows. As the deserts spread, the herds move on, devouring virtually everything as they go.

Once again it's a vicious circle. As the plants are eaten and the land dries up, weather patterns change and all rain virtually disappears. This ensures that once land has turned into desert it stays that way. Today, all around the globe, one-third of the world's surface is on the point of turning to desert because of overgrazing, according to the United Nations. It's a heck of a price to pay for a food we don't even need.

Unfortunately, meat producers don't have to pay the costs of clearing up the pollution they cause: no one charges pig breeders for the damage caused by their acid rain or beef producers for the useless land they create. However, the Centre for Science & the Environment, in New Delhi, India, has looked at different foods and put a real value on them, which includes these hidden costs. They reckon the price of a hamburger should be about £140. You'd need a lot of clowns to sell them at that price – and a lot of clowns to buy them!

Most people know very little about the food they eat and the damage much of it does to the environment. There's a Native American idea that life is like a spider's web, each strand made up of different things – animals, trees, rivers, oceans, insects and so on. If we destroy one of the strands we weaken the whole web. And that's what we have started to do.

So, going back to our evolutionary year, with the clock's hands pointing to one minute to midnight, a lot depends on the next few seconds. According to many scientists, a timescale as short as this generation's lifespan will be vital in deciding whether the world as we know it survives or not. It's scary but we can all do something about it.

'I don't see any justification for being a carnivore. I believe that eating meat is tantamount to damning the planet.'
Heather Small, lead singer of M People

Chapter 11
Fishy Business

'I'm a vegetarian but I eat fish.' Have you ever heard anyone say that? I always want to ask them what they think a fish is — a distant relation of a carrot, second cousin to a cauliflower? They certainly won't grow in your greenhouse!

Poor old fish have always had the raw end of the deal and I'm sure it's because some bright spark came up with the notion that they don't feel pain. Just think about that for a minute. Fish have livers and stomachs, blood, eyes and ears — in fact most of the internal bits that we have — but they don't feel pain? Then why have they got a central nervous system, the thing responsible for carrying messages to and from the brain, including feelings of pain? Of course fish feel pain — it's part of the survival mechanism which has enabled them to last the tens of millions of years they have.

Despite their ability to feel, there are no rules or regulations governing the way fish are killed. You can do more or less what you want to them, and just about everyone does. Most are killed by being gutted with a knife, usually while they're still alive, or they're tossed into bins and allowed to suffocate in a totally alien environment.

To find out about fishing I once sailed on a trawler and I was disgusted at what I saw. I found lots of things upsetting but worst of all was what happened to a big, orange-speckled flat fish – a plaice. It was tossed into a bin with other flat fish and four hours later I literally heard it croaking. I pointed it out to one of the deck-hands who, without even thinking about it, clubbed the fish. It was, I thought, better than suffocating and I presumed it had been killed. Six hours later I noticed that its mouth and gill covers were still opening and closing as it struggled for oxygen. Its misery had lasted ten hours.

Every possible method of catching fish has been thought of and used. In the boat I sailed on, a big, heavy, open-mouthed net called a trawl was used. Heavy boards keep the net on the sea bed and as they are pulled along, they crunch and grind over the sand, killing hundreds of different life forms. As the fish caught in the nets are brought up from the ocean depths, their swim bladders may burst or their eyes balloon out because of the difference in pressure. Often fish 'drown' because they are so crushed in the net under the weight of other fish that their gills can't work. As well as the fish that are caught, many other creatures are netted – including starfish, crabs and shell fish. These are simply shovelled back into the sea to die. Despite this, trawling is one of the most common methods of fishing in the world today.

There are some rules governing fishing – mainly about such things as the size of fishing nets and who can fish where. These are made by individual countries about their own coastal waters. Countries also have rules about how many and which types of fish can be caught. They call them fish quotas. It may sound like a sensible way of making sure that not too many fish are caught, but in fact it's nothing of the sort. It's just a crude attempt to share out what fish there are left.

In Europe, fish quotas work like this: let's take haddock and cod as an example. When a boat has caught all the haddock the rules allow, it's supposed to stop fishing for them but it can continue fishing for cod. As cod and haddock usually swim together, when the net is hauled in there will be haddock in it as well as cod. What the captain sometimes does is hide these illegal haddock in secret parts of the boat. More likely, they'll be thrown back in the sea. But there's one big problem – they're already dead! It's estimated that about 40 per cent more haddock than the quota allows are killed in this way. Unfortunately, it isn't just haddock which are affected by these crazy rules. It affects every species of fish covered by the quota system.

In the big, open oceans of the world or around the coasts of poorer countries, there are very few controls. In fact, there are so few regulations that something called biomass fishing has suddenly appeared. In this type of fishing, very fine mesh nets scoop every living thing from the water. Not even the smallest fish or tiniest crab survives.

All over the Southern oceans, a new and particularly disgusting type of fishing called finning has also come to light. Sharks are the target and when they're caught their fins are cut from them while they're still alive. Then the fish are dropped back into the sea to die of shock and drowning. This happens to over 100 million sharks every year. And all for shark's fin soup, sold in Chinese restaurants all over the world.

Another common method of fishing involves purse seine nets. These nets are used to form a circle around huge shoals and scoop out every single fish. The size of the mesh may allow the smallest fish to escape but so many adult fish are caught that the ones that are left can't breed fast enough to make up the loss. Sadly, this type of fishing also frequently catches dolphins and other sea mammals. Other methods of fishing include long lining, where thousands of baited hooks are attached to lines stretching several kilometres. These can be used over rocky sea beds which would tear a net to pieces. Explosives and poisons such as bleach are all part of the onslaught on the oceans and these too kill many more creatures than fish.

Probably the most destructive of all fishing methods, however, is drift netting. Made from thin but strong nylon, these nets are almost invisible in the water and dangle from the surface to form what have been called 'walls of death'. This name came about because of the large number of creatures which swim into the nets and die – dolphins, small whales, seals, sea birds, rays and sharks. They are all discarded because the only thing the fishermen are really after is tuna fish. Over a million dolphins alone die every year because of drift nets – drowned because they are unable to get to the surface to breathe.

Drift nets are now used all over the world and have recently appeared in Britain and Europe, where the nets are limited to about 2.5 kilometres in length. Out in the middle of big oceans such as the Pacific and the Atlantic, where few controls exist, nets can stretch for 30 kilometres or more. Sometimes these long nets break free during a storm and drift around, continuing to catch and kill animals. Finally, when the net is weighed down with dead bodies, it sinks to the sea bed. Over time, the bodies rot away and then the net floats back up to the surface of the ocean to continue its pointless destruction.

Nearly 100 million tons of fish are dragged from the sea by commercial fishing fleets every year, many caught before they're even old enough to breed, guaranteeing that the oceans cannot replenish themselves. And every year the situation gets worse. Every time someone – such as the United Nations Food and Agriculture Organisation (UNFAO) – gives another warning about the damage being done it's just ignored. Everyone knows the seas are dying but no one wants to be the first to stop fishing – there's just too much money involved.

Since World War Two, the world's seas and oceans have been divided up into 17 fishing areas. Today, nine of these 'are facing catastrophic declines in some species', says the UNFAO. The remaining eight areas are almost as bad, mostly due to overfishing.

The International Council for Exploration of the Seas (ICES) – the world's leading scientific expert on the seas and oceans – is also extremely worried about what's happening. It says that the huge shoals of mackerel which used to swim around the North Sea are now commercially extinct – not enough exist for fishermen to catch and sell. It also warns that in another five years one of the most common European species of all, the cod, will be entirely extinct. All of which is fine – if you like jelly fish. Because that, they fear, is all that will remain.

What's even worse is that much of the time, the animals taken from the seas don't even end up on someone's plate. They are turned into fertilisers to make crops grow or used to make shoe polish or candles. They're also used to feed to farm animals, including farmed fish. Can you believe that? We catch masses of fish, process them, turn them into pellets and feed them to other fish! It takes about 4 pounds of wild fish to produce a pound of farmed fish, the other 3 pounds being pooed away.

Some people think farming fish is the answer to the ocean's problems but it's as destructive as fishing. Millions of fish are packed into cages on the coastlines of the world's oceans, and coastal mangrove swamps are being cut down at a terrifying rate to make way for these farms. In places such as the Philippines, Kenya, India and Thailand, more than 70 per cent of the country's mangrove forests have gone – and they're still cutting.

Yet mangrove forests are so rich in life that over 2000 different plants and animals live in them. They are also the breeding grounds for 80 per cent of the world's marine fish species. These amazing areas are the nurseries of the seas and as they die, the oceans die too.

The fish farms which replace them pollute the water, covering the sea bed with uneaten food pellets and excreta which smothers all life. Cramming fish into cages makes them vulnerable to the spread of disease, so the fish are given antibiotics while insecticides are used to kill parasites such as sea lice. After just a few years, the environment is so badly damaged that the fish farms have to move on, cutting down more mangroves as they go.

In Norway and Britain – mostly in the fjords and Scottish lochs – fish farms are used for raising Atlantic salmon. In its natural state, this free-swimming fish roams far and wide, from tiny mountain streams to the deep Atlantic ocean off Greenland. It is so powerful that it can leap over waterfalls or swim directly up cascading water. Humans have tried to breed these instincts out of the salmon and have imprisoned it in metal pens in its millions.

All the problems of pollution apply to salmon farming just as they do to fish farming elsewhere in the world, and all add their bit to the demise of our seas.

As the seas and oceans collapse, it isn't just humans who are affected. Just imagine what is happening to the birds, seals, dolphins and other creatures who need fish to live. They're already struggling to survive and their future looks fairly grim. So shouldn't we leave the fish for them?

'The environmental reasons for not eating fish are overwhelming.'

Michaela Strachan, TV presenter

'If I look at the amount of fish being vacuumed off the sea bed to provide fodder for humans and livestock it bewilders me. It's all so unneccessary.'

Jeff Banks, designer and *Clothes Show* presenter

Chapter 12
Don't Bug Me...

Have you ever experienced this? About 12 hours after eating chicken you start to feel sick. This grows into sharp pains that keep shooting from your stomach to your back. Then you get explosive diarrhoea – you can't hold it back and you're never off the loo. Now you're feeling really ill! You're hot and you start to vomit. This goes on for a few days and then you feel tired for a couple of weeks. You swear you will never eat chicken again!

If your answer is yes then you're probably one of the millions of people every year who've suffered from food poisoning. And the chances are that animal-based foods were the cause.

Ninety-five per cent of all food poisoning is from meat, egg and dairy products. Even the odd little 5 per cent from fruit and vegetables is usually because of contamination by meat or manure. The bugs in animals are more likely to infect us than the bugs in vegetables simply because animals are biologically more like us. Many of the bugs which live in the blood or cells of other animals can also live quite happily in ours.

The bugs that cause food poisoning are bacteria and are so small they can't be seen with the human eye. Some bacteria thrive and grow inside the living animals while others infect the meat after slaughter because of the way it's kept or handled. Either way, we are increasingly catching diseases from the meat we eat and it's becoming more difficult to cure them.

Every week in Britain alone, over a thousand people go to their doctor with one kind of food poisoning or another according to government health figures. That adds up to about 85,000 cases a year, which you might think isn't that many out of a population of 58 million. But here's the catch! Scientists estimate that the real number is actually ten to a hundred times more than this but people don't bother to report it, they just stay at home and suffer. That's at least 850,000 cases of food poisoning every year, from which about 260 people die.

The bacteria responsible for all this suffering have names that read like a medical dictionary but here are the ones most likely to infect you. Salmonella is responsible for about a hundred deaths a year in Britain and is found mostly in fresh chickens, eggs, ducks and turkeys. It leads to diarrhoea and stomach pains.

Another real nasty found mostly in chicken and other poultry is campylobacter. It's the one I described at the beginning of the chapter – in fact it's the most common form of food poisoning of all, but kills very few.

Listeria also kills about a hundred people a year and is found in processed and chilled foods – cooked chicken, salamis, soft cheeses and cook-chilled meals. It's particularly bad for pregnant women and the flu-like symptoms can lead to blood poisoning and meningitis or even the death of the baby.

E.coli is known as the 'burger bug' because it thrives in burgers, mince and beef sausages. At the moment about fifty people a year die from it but it's on the increase and it's getting harder to stop. Doctors are so worried by it that it's now being referred to as a superbug. It causes enteritis (inflammation of the intestines) and can lead to kidney failure.

One of the reasons it's so difficult to control all the bacteria found in meat is that these bugs are constantly changing through a process called mutation. It's the equivalent of evolution in animals – the only difference is that bugs do it much faster, in hours rather than centuries. Lots of these mutated bugs die out quickly but others are amazingly successful. Some even manage to fight off the medicines which used to kill their ancestors. When this happens, scientists have to find new drugs or treatments.

Since 1947, when penicillin and other drugs called antibiotics were discovered, doctors have been able to treat most infections caused by bacteria, including food poisoning. What seems to be happening now is that the bacteria have changed and they've learned how to avoid being killed by antibiotics. With one type of the E. coli infection there are virtually no drugs which will kill it. And it's this which is worrying doctors because there are so few new drugs to take the place of the old ones which no longer work.

One of the reasons for the spread of bacteria in the meat we eat is the way animals are treated in slaughterhouses. The lack of hygiene, the water sloshing around all over the place, the roaring chainsaws that slice through carcasses showering blood, fat and bits of muscle and bone everywhere, all help to scatter bugs like confetti on a windy day. Professor Richard Lacey, a man who spends his working life investigating food poisoning, says: 'When a perfectly healthy, bug-free animal goes into a slaughterhouse there is a good chance it will come out as a disease-ridden carcass.'

Because of its link with heart disease and cancers and because of worries about E. coli, more and more people are giving up beef, lamb and pork and are turning to chicken as the healthier choice. Healthier? In some food processing plants such as meat-pie factories, chicken preparation areas are separated off from the rest by big glass screens. The fear is that other meats might be infected by the chicken – that's how bug-ridden it is.

In Britain, the government reckons that 43 per cent of all chicken meat is infected with the bacteria called salmonella. In fact, university tests show the number is actually much higher than this. Most birds naturally have small amounts of salmonella in their gut along with other bacteria. Because of the risk of disease in the sheds in which they're reared, chickens are fed antibiotics every day. This kills off some disease bacteria that might otherwise spread through the flock. How-

91

ever, it allows other bacteria to flourish and grow. Salmonella is one of these bacteria, and while it doesn't harm the chickens it ain't too good for us humans.

The way chickens are processed after they're killed practically guarantees that salmonella and other bugs such as campylobacter, are spread from one bird to another. After throat cutting, the birds are dunked in the same scalding tank. The temperature of the water is about 50°C, hot enough to loosen their feathers but not hot enough to kill bacteria, which breed in the water.

The next step in the process is just as bad. The intestines of any animal are teeming with bugs. With slaughtered chickens, the intestines are removed automatically with the same spoon-shaped tool. It scoops out the insides of one bird after another — every bird on the production line — spreading disease as it does so. Even when the chicken carcasses go into the freezer, the bacteria aren't killed, just prevented from breeding and increasing. But as soon as the meat is defrosted, the bugs start to breed again.

The official story is that if chicken is cooked properly there isn't a health problem because the salmonella will be killed — and there's a lot of truth in this. But it's not the full story because when you unwrap an uncooked chicken or chicken pieces, you will almost certainly get salmonella on your hands and this bacteria can grow on almost anything else you touch, even work surfaces.

The way meat is handled in shops can also cause problems. I remember listening once to someone who worked in a supermarket talking about her work. She said the thing she hated most was the 'peppermint creams'. I couldn't think what she meant until she explained that peppermint creams were the little round, creamy-looking, bacteria-ridden, pus-filled abscesses which they often came across when they were cutting up meat. And what did they do with them? Well, they simply scraped away the pus, cut that particular piece of meat off and chucked it in the bin. The waste bin? No, the mince bin!

There are plenty of other ways you can eat diseased meat without even realising it. Over the last few years, all kinds of discoveries have been made by newspaper and television journalists about the way in which meat is treated. Poor old cows, passed as unfit for human consumption because of disease or because they're full of drugs, have finished up in meat pies and other products. Of course it's illegal and the meat is dyed bright green to stop this kind of thing, but it sometimes fails. (So what you thought was parsley in your meat pie . . .)

There have also been cases where supermarkets have returned meat to their suppliers because it had gone off, and all the suppliers did was cut off the pieces which looked bad, washed the rest, then chopped it up and resold it as fresh, lean meat. You can't tell if meat is okay just by looking at it. Why do suppliers do it? Let the Head of the Environmental Health Institute give you the answer: 'Imagine the profits that can be made from buying a dead, condemned animal for £25 and selling it on as fit meat worth at least £600 in the shops.'

No one knows how widespread this practice is but

on the evidence of those who have investigated it, it is widespread and getting worse. The most worrying thing about all this is that the poorest, cheapest and often most diseased meat finishes up being sold to those who buy in bulk as cheaply as possible – hospitals, old people's homes and schools, where it finishes up in dinners.

A new, frightening disease is caused by the 'thing' which causes mad cow disease or, to give it its proper name, bovine spongiform encephalopathy – BSE for short. The reason I say 'thing' is because scientists don't know *what* it is. There are all kinds of theories about what the BSE bug might be and the most common is that it is a prion – a weird bit of protein that can change its form, one minute being as lifeless as a grain of sand and the next being alive, active and deadly. But no one knows for sure.

Scientists aren't even sure how this thing suddenly appeared in cows. Some say it was caught from sheep, who have a similar type of disease, but others disagree. One thing over which there is no argument is how it spreads. BSE is common in Britain because it was there that cattle, who left alone would eat nothing but grass, plants and leaves, were given ground-up bits of other cattle and sheep in their feed, including brains in which the bug is thought to have been present. In this way, the disease spreads.

There is no cure for BSE. It kills cows and it can kill other types of animals such as cats, mink and even deer who are fed the infected beef. There is a similar human disease called CJD (Creutzfeldt-Jakob Disease) and there has been a big argument over whether this is the same as BSE and whether humans can catch it from eating BSE infected beef and other bits of cows. For ten years after BSE was first discovered in 1986, the British government said humans couldn't catch it and that CJD was a different disease – therefore beef was perfectly safe to eat. As a precaution, they eventually said that brains, certain glands and the nerves which run through the spine shouldn't be eaten. Previously these bits had been ground up and used in things like burgers, pies and stock cubes.

Between 1986 and 1996, at least 160,000 British cows were known to have caught BSE. These animals were destroyed and not used for human food. However, one scientist estimates that a further 1.5 million cattle were also infected but didn't exhibit any symptoms. Even the UK government's own figures show that for every cow with BSE that they knew about, there were two more they didn't. These cattle, although infected, were all eaten.

In March 1996, the British government had to make an admission. They said that it looked as though they had been wrong and humans *could* catch BSE from cattle after all. This is a frightening mistake to have made because millions of people have eaten infected meat. There was even a four-year period before food manufacturers were told not to use brains and nerves, when these highly infectious parts of cattle were being eaten regularly.

Even after admitting its mistake, the government still insisted that it had made sure all the dangerous parts of cattle were being removed and that it was therefore safe for people to go on eating beef. But in a recorded telephone conversation, the chief vet of the Meat & Livestock Commission – the national organisation responsible for selling red meat – admitted that the BSE bug is in all beef meat, even lean steaks. It might only be present in small quantities but no one knows what effect eating small quantities of infected meat over a long period of time will have. All we know now is that it takes between 10 and 30 years for humans to show the symptoms of BSE or CJD and it always ends in death after a year or so.

You will be pleased to hear that I don't know of anyone who has ever died of carrot poisoning.

The World's First Literary Reference to BSE?

Sir Andrew Aguecheeck: Methinks sometimes I have no more wit than a Christian or an ordinary man has: but I am a great eater of beef and I believe that does harm my wit.
Sir Toby: No question.

From *Twelfth Night* by William Shakespeare

Section 3
Meat: The Mighty Myth

Introduction

What nationality you are, how you speak, many of the things you believe in and what you eat are really an accident of where you were born. An Austrian might be crazy about skiing but if they'd been born in the USA it could have been baseball. You might like thick butter on your bread but if you'd been Italian it would have been olive oil. Most Europeans and Americans eat meat regularly — you might still do — but had you been born a Hindu in India, you wouldn't know what it tastes like.

So, we have to be very careful when we use words like 'natural' or 'we're meant to' or 'it's human nature'. What might be 'natural', 'necessary' or 'instinctive' for one person is entirely the opposite for another.

Most people in the rich countries of the world are often told that it's natural to eat meat. What does this mean? That we're born meat eaters, that we're biologically programmed to do it, that our instinct tells us to kill animals? But let's put this to the test. Let your imagination run free for a minute.

Visualise a young cat in a small enclosed space with a mouse. It will immediately leap on the mouse and bat it around until it's dead. In the wild it would then eat it. Now imagine a small child in an enclosed space with a lamb. The child will almost certainly stroke the lamb, play with it or hold it. I don't think you'll find many children trying to kill it!

Okay, it's not the most scientific approach but I think you get the message. The next five chapters are all about who tells us it's right to eat meat and why they do it. The best bit is, it also shows you why they're wrong.

Of all the objections and finger wagging you're ever likely to get as a vegetarian, most will be about the information in this section. So read on!

Special Bonus Fact

Vegetarianism is not a new idea and certainly not a fad!
Check out what these geniuses from the past
(forgiving their sexism!) had to say:

'The day will come when men look upon
the murder of animals as we now look upon
the murder of men.'
Leonardo da Vinci, 1452–1519, artist (painted *The Mona Lisa*),
scientist, musician, sculptor, prolific inventor and great
animal rights campaigner

'As long as men massacre animals, they
will kill each other. Indeed he who sows the
seed of murder and pain cannot reap
joy and love.'
Pythagoras, 6th century BC, ancient Greek philosopher and
ace at maths (yes, it was him who discovered all that
stuff about triangles!)

'Animals are my friends and I don't
eat my friends.'
George Bernard Shaw, 1856–1950, the great Irish playwright
(works include *Pygmalion*, made into the musical *My Fair Lady*,
Heartbreak Hotel and *Saint Joan*)

'Our task must be to free ourselves...
by widening our circle of compassion to
embrace all living creatures and the whole of
nature in its beauty.'
Albert Einstein, 1879–1955, genius physicist (he said $E=MC^2$)
and vegetarian

Chapter 13
Political Persuasion

Having read this far there is probably a question which you're dying to ask. Why, if meat is as bad as all the evidence shows, don't governments do something about it? It's a good question but not that easy to answer.

First, politicians aren't gods, they're ordinary human beings. Whichever party they belong to, their first aim is to gain or keep power. Without power, politicians can do nothing. So the first lesson of politics is – don't upset the people who have money and influence and who can take your power away from you. The second lesson is – don't go around telling the majority of the population things they don't want to hear, even if they may need to know it. If you do, they will simply vote for someone else.

The meat industry is big and powerful and most

people don't want to be told the truth about meat eating. And those are two reasons why governments say nothing.

Meat and dairy production is by far the biggest and wealthiest side of farming and a huge industry. The value of Britain's cattle alone is around £20 billion and before the BSE scandal in 1996, UK exports of beef added up to £3 billion every year. Then add to that all the chicken, pork and turkey growers and all the companies who make things out of meat – burgers, pies, sausages and so on. We are talking mega amounts of money! Any government that started telling people not to eat meat would jeopardise the profits of these corporations and they would use their power against it. This advice would also be extremely unpopular with the general public; just think how many people you know who eat meat. That, I'm afraid, is a simple statement of fact.

Governments everywhere tend to see environmental destruction, starvation in the South and even human health as long-term problems which they don't have to worry about too much now. Spending large amounts of money on these things doesn't help to get them re-elected. Only when ordinary people know the facts and start to demand change will anything happen.

The meat industry also spends a vast amount of money advertising directly to the public, telling them every day in every way that meat is good, necessary and natural. On British television there have been the *Meat to Live* and *Meat the Language of Love* advertisements paid for by the Meat & Livestock Commission out of its annual £42 million marketing and advertising budget. The poultry industry advertises chickens, ducks and turkeys. Then there are the hundreds of individual companies too that make profits out of meat: Sun Valley and Birds Eye chicken, McDonalds and Burger King burgers, Bernard Matthews turkey, Matteson's cold meats, Danish bacon – the list is almost endless and the amount of money involved huge. I'll give you one example – McDonalds. Every year they sell burgers worth US$26 billion in 18,000 restaurants in 89 countries. And the message is constant: Meat is okay!

Ever heard the story of Pinnochio, about a wooden puppet who comes to life and tells whoppers? Every time he lies his nose grows a bit longer until he finishes up with a huge conk. The story was meant as a warning to children not to tell lies. It should have been written for some of the adults who sell meat, and this is why.

Producers will tell you that their pigs are much happier living inside in their warm pens where they get plenty of food and don't have to worry about the rain and cold. But as anyone who's read Chapter 1 will know, this is an outright lie. Factory-farmed pigs are so stressed out and bored that they often go mad.

The egg section in my local supermarket has a phoney thatched roof with phoney chickens. When little kids pull a string, a recording of a clucking hen plays. On the egg boxes it says 'Farm Fresh' or 'Country Fresh' and there's a picture of chicken in a field. This is the 'Fooled you' lie! Without saying so, the egg producers have made you think that chickens wander around as free as . . . well, a bird. (As we've seen in Chapter 3 that just isn't true.)

'Meat to Live' says the advertisement. That's what I call the 'half-a-story' lie. Of course you *can* live with meat as part of your diet but how much of it would they sell if they told the full story: 'Meat for 40 per cent more cancers' or 'Meat for 50 per cent more heart disease' which as Chapter 16 shows is the complete truth.

But why would anyone tell such fibs? The answer, my veggie or soon-to-be-veggie friend, is easy – money! The moment loads-a-money can be made from something, is the time when truth is in danger of taking a back seat. As for the animals which suffer – well, animals can't vote, can they?

If it sounds like I'm being unfair to politicians then just think about cigarettes. Tobacco is the biggest killer in the world and now plays a part in one half of all deaths around the globe. It's been known to cause cancer and other diseases for over 30 years. In fact most people who smoke want to stop but find it very hard because tobacco is an extremely powerful drug.

So what do governments do about it? There's no really serious campaign to say don't smoke; cigarettes are still advertised in high streets all over the world and in almost every newspaper and magazine; you can buy them everywhere and they're cheap enough for anyone to get hold of. Why? Could it be the billions of pounds which governments make every year in taxation on tobacco?!

So you see, when money's involved the truth may be hidden or sometimes even buried completely. But it can't be taken away from you once you have it. And truth is also power because the more you know the less easily you can be fooled.

> **'The greatness of a nation and its moral progress can be judged by the way it treats its animals...The only way to live is to let live.'**
>
> Mahatma Gandhi, 1869–1948, Indian peace activist

> **'The more we know about the meat industry the more we can do to stop it. Knowledge really is power.'**
>
> Damon Albarn, lead singer of Blur

Chapter 14
Meat is Macho

'There's no hope for my dad!' is the most common complaint from young, would-be veggies. When trying to go veggie, it's nearly always dads who are the most difficult, the least understanding and the ones who object the loudest. After you've gone veggie you often find that mums are more willing to listen to the arguments, and sometimes become veggie themselves.

If mums do complain, it's more often because they're worried about the inconvenience and not knowing what to cook. But too many dads seem unmoved by the plight of animals, and as for giving up meat – you must be joking! So why the difference?

There's an old saying which you sometimes hear parents repeating to their little boys when they've hurt themselves; 'Big boys don't cry!' Given half a chance, they certainly do. So is it that men and women are made differently or is it because men have been taught to behave the way they do?

Right from the time they're born, some boys are encouraged to be macho by their parents. You don't hear grown ups saying to little girls, 'Who's a big strong girl, then?' or, 'Who's my little soldier?' And as boys get older, the same sort of macho expectations continue.

Just think of the names used to describe boys who don't seem to be macho enough — weed, cissy and some even nastier. They're often used when a boy hasn't been 'tough enough' or has shown that he's frightened. Sometimes it's even because a boy has shown he cares about something.

As boys grow up there are other expressions that describe the way they're supposed to act — stiff upper lip, not letting the side down, not being 'hen pecked'. When all these sayings and expressions are put together over a person's lifetime, they become a constant drip, drip, drip of pressure telling men how to behave.

Men, according to these old-fashioned messages, must hide their feelings and emotions and not show what they really think. If you believe this baloney then being a man means being hard and unemotional. It means rejecting things like compassion and concern as 'soft' and it means never showing that you care.

Of course not all men are like this. There are male vegans, vegetarians and animal rights activists who are the opposite of this unfeeling image. I've spoken to some who used to fit into this macho image but who eventually rejected it. One friend of mine used to shoot birds, rabbits and other wildlife. He says that every time he looked at the creatures he'd killed, he felt guilty. He felt particularly bad when he had only injured something and it had escaped, probably to die alone and in pain. That feeling of guilt worried him.

His real concern, however, was that he saw his feelings as a sign of weakness – not very manly. He felt sure that if he carried on shooting and killing things, one day he'd be able to do it without the worrying, nagging sense of being cruel. Then at last he would be just like all the other hunters he knew. Of course he didn't really know how they felt because, just like him, they never expressed their feelings. It wasn't until another bloke said to him that it was perfectly okay not to want to kill animals that he was able to admit to himself that he didn't like hunting.

The answer was simple – he didn't go shooting again and he stopped eating meat so no one else had to kill animals for him.

Most dads it seems, even if they've never picked up a shotgun in their lives, have some of this confusion in them. Part of the answer might be somewhere way back in our history.

Early humans lived as hunter-gatherers but hunting wasn't just a way of providing extra food. In fact hunting was often a very poor and inefficient way of feeding the family. Instead, killing animals became tied up with masculinity and being physically brave. In the Masai tribe in East Africa, for instance, a young man wasn't considered a full warrior until he'd killed a lion all by himself.

The real business of providing food usually fell to women, who gathered fruits, berries, nuts and seeds.

In other words, they were the ones who did most of the work. (Not a lot changes, does it?) It seems that hunting was the modern equivalent of all the boys getting together in the pub or going to a football match. The same attitude seems to have carried on right up until today.

There is another reason why more men eat meat than women, and it comes out every time I talk to a group of young blokes. They really think that eating meat, particularly red meat, helps to build their muscles. Many of them believe that without it they will be puny and physically weak. Of course the elephant, rhinoceros and gorilla are great examples of what happens if you eat only veggie food.

All this might account for why there are twice as many vegetarian women than men and why women are often belittled for it. If you're a vegetarian or vegan young woman then be prepared for the following insults — including from some dads. It's only because you're female — therefore over-emotional. You're not being rational — which is another way of saying that caring is wrong. It's because you're impressionable — in other words a bit soft. You don't know the facts — because science is for men. What they're really saying is that you aren't behaving like a 'sensible' (unemotional), 'clear thinking' (unfeeling) man! Now, did you ever need a better reason to go or stay veggie?

Vegetarianism is for wimps?
No way!

Martina Navratilova, legendary tennis champion with 166 titles and nine times Wimbledon winner – **vegetarian.**

Robert Millar, world-class cyclist and winner at the Tour of Britain, fourth in the Tour de France, and second at the Tours of France, Spain, Italy and Switzerland – **vegetarian.**

Ed Moses, twice gold medallist at the Olympics for 400m hurdles – **vegetarian.**

Sorya Bonall, world-champion ice skater – **vegan.**

Mr Muscle Man himself – **Dave Scott**, six times winner of the Ironman Triathlon of the USA – **vegetarian.**

Sally Hibberd, UK Mountain Bike champion – **vegetarian.**

Judy Leden, European and world hang-gliding champion – **vegetarian.**

Carl Lewis, world-class sprinter – **vegan.**

Chapter 15
But We're *Meant* to Eat Meat

The most boring reply in the world when you tell someone you're a vegetarian is, 'But we're meant to eat meat!' Let's get it straight right now, we are *not* meant to eat meat. Humans are not carnivores like cats; we're not even omnivores like a pig or a bear.

If you really think you're meant to eat meat, try running into a field, jumping on the back of a cow and biting it! You wouldn't even be able to get your teeth or your fingernails through its skin. Or try picking up a dead chicken and chomping on it; we just don't have the teeth for eating meat without cooking it first.

We are, in fact, herbivores — and that doesn't mean a creature like a cow with four stomachs that spends all day munching grass. Cows are ruminants; herbivores eat a whole range of vegetable foods, like nuts, seeds, roots, shoots, fruits and berries. How do I know this? Because numerous studies have been done on what apes eat. The gorilla, for example, is entirely vegan.

An eminent doctor, David Ryde, one-time medical adviser to the British Olympic Association, once tried a little experiment. He displayed two pictures at a medical exhibition. One was of a human's intestines; the other of a gorilla's intestines. He then asked his colleagues to look at them and make any comments. All the doctors present thought both pictures were of human beings and not one identified the gorilla.

I know it doesn't go with Nike trainers, Benetton jumpers and Oxy-10 spot remover, but that's what we are – apes. Over 98 per cent of our genes are the same as a chimpanzee's and any visitor from space trying to work out what type of animal we are would immediately classify us as a type of chimp. They're our nearest relative. Terrible that, when you think of the disgusting things we do to them in laboratories.

A good indicator of what our diet would naturally be is to watch our ape relatives in the wild. They are almost entirely vegan. Some eat a little meat in the form of termites or maggots (very tasty) but this accounts for a tiny part of their overall diet. A scientist called Jane Goodall lived in the jungle alongside chimps and studied them for ten years. She made a note of everything they ate and was able to show exactly how much of it was meat – it was the equivalent amount to a pea a day. So little, in fact, that their teeth and gut are those of a vegan.

However, the 'we're meant to eat meat' brigade got very excited when naturalist David Attenborough showed a film on TV of one particular group of chimpanzees hunting and eating colubus monkeys. They said this was proof that we're natural meat eaters.

There is no real explanation for this group of chimps but they seem to be the exception. Most chimpanzees don't go looking for meat and never pick up frogs and lizards or other small creatures from the forest floor, although they are there for the taking. It's thought that their liking for termites and maggots is because of their sweet taste.

A good way of telling what an animal is supposed to eat is by looking at its body. An ape's teeth, like ours, is made up mostly of flat surfaces for crushing and grinding. Our jaws are also designed to move from side to side to help this process. Both these characteristics are the signs of a mouth designed to cope with tough, vegetable foods full of fibre.

Because foods of this type are difficult to digest, the process starts as soon as the food is in the mouth when it's mixed with saliva. The chewed up mass then passes through the body very slowly, snaking its way through the long intestines so all the nutrients can be absorbed.

Meat eaters, like cats, are built completely differently. Not only does a cat have claws to grab hold of its prey but its teeth are sharp, with no flat surfaces. Its jaw can only move up and down in a chopping motion and the animal bolts its food down in big chunks. It doesn't need a cookery book and British Gas to help digest it either.

The inside of a carnivore's stomach is a bubbling mass of acid that would take the paint off a car. It's designed to break the meat down quickly so the poisons, released by the meat as it decays, don't hang around too long. Its intestines are short, about three times the length of its body when stretched out in one line, and are designed to get the waste out of the body as quick as possible.

Imagine what would happen to a piece of meat if you left it on a window sill on a sunny day. It wouldn't take long before it began to rot and produce poisonous toxins. This process can also happen inside the body which is why animals which are meant to eat meat get rid of the waste as quickly as possible. Human digestion is much slower because our intestines are about 12 times the length of our bodies. This is thought to be one reason why colon cancer is much higher in meat eaters than in vegetarians.

Obviously humans did start eating meat at some time in history, but for the majority of people in the world right up into this century, meat was a comparatively rare food and most people ate it only three or four times a year, usually at big religious festivals. It's only really since the Second World War that people started eating meat in such huge amounts – which may explain why heart disease and cancers have suddenly become the biggest killers of all known diseases. One by one, all the excuses used by meat eaters to justify their diet have been demolished. The weakest one of all is that we're meant to eat meat!

Chapter 16
The Healthiest Diet on Earth

What do you think would happen if you ate nothing but meat — all kinds of meat — and dairy products? You'd die, probably within a year. What would happen if you ate nothing but a varied vegan or vegetarian diet including fruit, veg, beans, grains, nuts and seeds? You'd probably be much healthier than most people are today.

That has to be the starting point for understanding what is and what isn't a good diet. So, if anyone ever tells you that meat is vital for life, you can be certain they don't know what they're talking about. You know the sort of thing, someone who smokes like a chimney suddenly becomes a world authority on health when it comes to vegetarianism.

Health is generally the biggest worry of non-veggie parents when young people decide to give up meat.

Parents often think you're going to fade away or be stricken by an army of diseases without your daily dose of dead animal protein. In fact, they should be really pleased because all the evidence suggests that veggies are usually much healthier than meat-eaters.

All the latest reports, including one by the World Health Organisation, say that people on a meat-based diet eat twice as much sugary and a third more fatty foods than is good for them. If you're between 11 and 16, the figures are even worse because meat-eaters in this age group eat three times as much of these unhealthy foods. A good example of a fatty, sugary meal is cola, burger and chips followed by ice cream. A staple diet of this kind is bad news both because of what's in the food and also because of what's *not* in it.

So let's start with the burger meal and look at what it contains that you don't need. Top of the list is saturated animal fat – and burgers contain a lot. The fat's minced up with the meat, even when it looks lean. It's also used in dairy products such as ice cream and often the chips are fried in it too, soaking up large amounts as they cook.

This doesn't mean that all fats are unhealthy – it just depends on what kind you eat. Basically, there are two main kinds of fat – unsaturated fats, found mostly in vegetable foods, and saturated fats, found mostly in animal-based foods. Unsaturated fats are better for the body than saturated fats and a certain amount are essential in everyone's diet. Saturated fats, on the other hand, aren't needed and perhaps one of the most important health discoveries of all time is that saturated animal fats are linked to heart disease.

Why is that so important? Because heart disease is now the biggest killer of men and women in the Western world. Meat, fish and dairy products also contain a substance called cholesterol and this together with the fats is helping to cause this epidemic. In contrast, unsaturated fats like olive oil, sunflower oil and corn oil actually help to reduce the artery clogging caused by animal fats.

As well as containing things that are bad for you, burgers – in fact all meat products – are lacking in things that you need. These substances include fibre and five extremely important vitamins.

Fibre is made up of the tough bits of fruit and vegetables that your body can't digest. It contains no nutrients and passes straight through the body, but despite that it's extremely important. Fibre gives the bowels something bulky to grip on to, and that helps them to work properly, forcing the waste food from the body. It seems that fibre acts like a brush, sweeping the bowels clean (now there's a lovely image). Too little fibre and the food takes longer to pass through our bowels, allowing poisons to infect the body. Lack of fibre combined with too much animal fat helps cause another killer disease – colon cancer.

Recent medical research has also identified three vitamins that actually help to protect people against about 60 diseases, including the big killers of heart disease, stroke and cancer. These are vitamins A (the type from plant foods only), C and E and they've been given the name antioxidants. These vitamins are the goodies. They work by wiping out molecules called free radicals (which are the baddies and not some fringe political group). Free radicals are constantly produced by the body as a result of breathing, exercise or even digestion. They're part of a process known as oxidation – the same process that causes metal to rust. These molecules don't make you rusty but act like out-of-control hooligans, dashing around the body crashing into cells and damaging them. Antioxidants mop up free radicals and stop them causing the damage which can lead to disease.

In 1996, over 200 studies confirm the amazing benefits of antioxidants. For example the National Cancer Institute and Harvard Medical School revealed that eating vitamins A, C and E from fresh fruit and veg reduced heart disease and cancer. These vitamins even help keep your brain active in old age!

However, none of these three antioxidants is in meat. Meat also contains little or no vitamins D, which controls the level of calcium in the blood, or K, which helps blood to clot. The only source of all these vital health protectors is fruit and veg, and sunlight, butter or margarine in the case of vitamin D.

Over the years, a huge number of scientific studies have also been carried out into how different diets in general affect people's well being. These studies have shown without doubt that vegetarian or vegan diets are the healthiest there are. Some of these studies have compared the diets of tens of thousands of people in places as far apart as China and America, Japan and Europe.

One of the biggest and most recent was carried out in Britain by Oxford University and the first results were published in 1995. The study looked at 11,000 people over a 13-year period and came to the staggering conclusion that vegetarians get 40 per cent less cancer of all kinds, 30 per cent less heart disease and are less likely to drop dead before reaching old age.

That same year, a group of doctors in the USA, called the Physicians Committee for Responsible Medicine, came up with an even more astounding result. They looked at over a hundred different pieces of research from around the world and on the basis of their findings came to the conclusion that vegetarians get up to 57 per cent less heart disease and up to 50 per cent less cancer of all kinds. They also found there were fewer cases of high blood pressure amongst vegetarians and in those who did have high blood pressure it tended to be less severe. Again, the improvement was estimated at up to 50 per cent.

To put worried parents' minds at rest, these doctors also found that the brains of young vegetarians developed quite normally. In fact at the age of 10, veggie kids tended to be a year more advanced mentally than meat eaters! So convincing were their arguments that the USA government has now accepted that 'Vegetarians have excellent health, obtain all the nutrients they need and vegetarianism is a suitable diet for US citizens.'

The usual meat-eaters' argument against this type of discovery is to say that veggies are healthier because they also tend to drink or smoke less and that this is why they do so well in these studies. Not true – as serious studies, like the ones I've written about here, always compare like with like. In other words they compare only non-drinking veggies with non-drinking meat-eaters, and so on.

None of this stops the meat industry from advertising meat as the healthiest food in the world. Although it obviously isn't, all their publicity may cause parents to worry. Believe me, meat producers don't sell meat to make people healthier, they do it to make a lot of money.

Okay, so what diseases do vegetarians get that meat eaters don't? None! Pretty amazing, eh?

'I became vegetarian for the animals but there were other unexpected benefits. I started to feel healthier — I became more supple which is important for an athlete. I also needed less sleep and woke up feeling much fresher. My skin improved and I had more energy. I love being vegetarian.'

Martina Navratilova, world tennis champion

Chapter 17
Nutrition in a Nutshell

When it comes to giving vegetarians advice on nutrition, most meat-eaters seem to think they're experts. They're usually not. In fact, few people *are* experts on the subject. Here, however, is nutrition made simple!

Protein is what people seem to worry about most when they go vegetarian. Concerned mums and dads say things like 'But what about your protein?' as though it was the most difficult substance in the world to find after diamonds. You do not need to worry about lack of protein, okay! In fact, you're more likely to be run down by stampeding hippopotami in your local high street than to meet a vegetarian suffering from a lack of protein.

Protein is important because it helps you grow. It repairs damage to your body and it also fights infection.

The good news is, it's in nearly all foods, including fruit and veg. The best source of protein is in what are known as pulses. These include chick peas and lentils as well as all the members of the bean family such as kidney beans, broad beans and even baked beans. The star bean when it comes to protein is the soya bean, which is used to make a whole range of veggie products including tofu, veggie burgers and sausages, soya milk and even something called TVP – textured vegetable protein – which is really not as bad as it sounds! Protein is also found in free-range eggs, cheese, nuts, seeds and even rice and pasta.

Protein is made up of different amino acids and some foods, such as soya products, milk, cheese and meat, contain all the amino acids. Other foods contain just some of them. Simply by eating different types of food together in a vegetarian or vegan diet you can ensure that different amino acids are combined and – bingo – perfect protein. This is something which every major nutritional organisation in the world agrees about. We don't even have to eat all these different foods in the same meal because our body can store amino acids until it needs them.

In its dietary guidelines published in 1995, the USA government made a special point of saying that vegetarians get all the protein they need. The British Medical Association, one of the most respected medical bodies in the world, said exactly the same thing several years before, and quite right too because *there has not been a single case of protein deficiency caused by going vegetarian or vegan in the Western world!* And that's why I say you don't need to worry.

Iron is another thing that parents sometimes get in a twist about – and with good reason. It's responsible for maintaining healthy red blood cells which carry oxygen to all parts of the body. A lack of iron, known as anaemia, means that your body and brain aren't getting enough oxygen, with the result that you feel constantly tired and run-down. It's one of the biggest dietary problems in Britain today, particularly amongst women who menstruate (have periods).

There is iron in meat but it's also found in a whole range of vegetarian foods including pulses, wholemeal bread, leafy green vegetables like spinach, dried fruits – particularly apricots and figs – and cocoa, which is a good excuse to pig out on plain chocolate! There's also iron in pasta, pumpkin and sesame seeds, pistachio and cashew nuts, fortified breakfast cereals and jacket potatoes.

Again, the British Medical Association insists that 'iron deficiency is no more common' in vegetarians and vegans than it is in meat-eaters. Scientists at the University of Surrey have also studied the health of British vegans. They state in the *British Journal of Nutrition* that iron levels 'were normal in all the vegans' and that children reared on vegan diets were perfectly healthy. In fact, anaemia may often result because the body has a problem absorbing iron rather than because a person isn't eating enough. Vitamin C helps you absorb iron and fortunately veggies and vegans tend to get a lot of this as it's in most green veg, potatoes, tomatoes and citrus fruits. It's even added to cartons of orange juice and instant potatoes.

New veggies often worry about lack of **calcium** –

they needn't. Going veggie – giving up meat and fish but still eating milk, cheese, butter and other dairy products – will make no difference because there's hardly any calcium in meat. Calcium gives healthy teeth and bones and helps the muscles work. As well as dairy products, calcium's found in nuts and seeds, pulses, leafy green veg and fortified soya milk. So, vegans also manage absolutely fine.

A varied vegetarian or vegan diet contains every **vitamin and mineral** you need, so don't let anyone tell you that by giving up meat you'll go short of them. Each vitamin and mineral performs a different task and most can be stored by the body so they don't have to be eaten every day, the main exception being vitamin C.

It was the lack of this vitamin that caused sailors on long sea voyages to die from a disease called scurvy in the old sailing-ship days when they ran out of fresh fruit and vegetables. Because they didn't have refrigeration, sailors in those days would eat the mould that grew on bread just to get some fresh greens! However because it's in almost all fresh produce, vitamin C is almost certain to be a daily part of your diet without going to such lengths! Officially, you need very little vitamin C every day to remain healthy but the more that's found out about it, the more important vitamin C seems to be in fighting disease. So the advice has got to be, eat plenty of fresh fruit and veg.

One vitamin that veggies and vegans are often asked about is **vitamin B12**, which is produced by bugs in the soil. Our ancestors used to obtain this vitamin by eating vegetables with bits of soil left on them. These days vegetarians get all they need of this vitamin from eating dairy products while vegans are amply supplied by fortified foods such as soya milk, TVP and most breakfast cereals. Yeast extract such as Marmite, Vecon and Vegemite is also a good source. Our liver can store B12 for years and only minute traces are needed – the equivalent to one-millionth of a gram per day. So you can pig out one day and eat none for days after.

What else might you be lacking if you give up meat? Nothing! For a start meat has no vitamin C and it has little or no vitamins D, K and E. Meat also has no beta carotene which our bodies process into vitamin A and which protects us from disease. In fact meat is very short of most vitamins. By eating a good variety of fruit, veg and pulses it's easy to get all the vitamins you need – just don't live on crisps and sweets!

On the other hand, **complex carbohydrates** are the one thing that almost no one talks about, as if they don't matter. Believe me they do. Complex carbohydrates are found in grains – including bread, pasta, rice, barley and rye – as well as root veg such as potatoes and yams. These carbohydrates are of *numero uno* importance because they supply the vital energy that your body needs to keep working properly.

Many people still think that eating complex carbohydrates make you fat and they try to cut down on them. A big mistake! Every health authority in every country, including the World Health Organisation, tells us to eat more of them. These are the things that should form the bulk of our diet. And do you know what? There's none in meat, which is why the average meat-eater doesn't get enough!

Fats and oils are also important. They help to

repair damaged tissues, produce some hormones and act as carriers for vitamins. Everyone needs a small amount of fats and oils and they occur naturally in most seeds and nuts and in some vegetables such as avocado – they don't just come in a bottle or packet. What your body doesn't need are the saturated fats that come from animals nor the cholesterol that accompanies them.

And now we come to the biggest question of all – what exactly *is* a balanced diet? The simple answer is to eat as wide a range of foods as possible. Include lots of carbohydrates and as many different vegetables and fruits as you can. Try the different pulses, dried fruits, mushrooms and specialist vegetarian products. You don't need to cram these all together in one meal or even every day – just be adventurous in what you eat.

It's fine to eat fast foods some of the time and to pig out occasionally on the things you like best. But the golden rule is this: the wider the range of foods you eat, the better your diet – and that's also the case for meat-eaters. It's also true that the less processed food is, the better the range of nutrients it contains. So, wholemeal bread and brown rice, for example, have more vitamins, minerals and fibre than the white versions. You can also get wholemeal pasta and noodles but personally I would sooner eat shredded cardboard!

It's taken a long time but at last the message is getting through that a vegetarian or vegan diet is healthier than a meat-based one. And as long as you're sensible about what you eat, your parents can rest happy that you're eating one of the best diets in the world!

Section 4
Standing Your Ground

Introduction

Up to now, we've looked at what happens to the animals that people eat. We've completely demolished the myths about vegetarianism and exposed the truth about the impact of meat-eating on the planet and on people's health.

But what about the practicalities of actually going, being and staying veggie? This section looks at how being veggie fits in with everything else in our lives, including the situation at home and at school with parents, teachers and friends.

When I first became a vegetarian, I couldn't believe it when I told people the truth about eating meat and they didn't seem to listen. Often it turned out that people believed what I was saying, but that they just didn't want to do anything about it. The good news is that these days more and more people *do* care and are changing — that's why vegetarianism is growing so rapidly all over the world. In Britain alone, over 5 million people are vegetarian or vegan — and over half a million of them are under 18 years old.

All the same, if you've never been veggie before, it can feel like a big step. What impact will it have on what you eat, what you do, who you do it with and where you hang out? Never fear! We look at the first steps for virgin veggies in the first chapter of this section.

And if you're veggie already, this section also gives the low-down on how to explain and convince others of your point of view. (Happily, the days of young people being seen but not heard have long gone!) It also explores some common dilemmas — like whether or not to snog a meatie — and looks at the best ways of dealing with aggro . . . whoever it's from! Best of all this section helps you make the most of what you know and gives you all the support you need to stand up for what you believe.

Chapter 18
First Steps for Virgin Veggies

So you've decided to go veggie or vegan – now what do you do? Panic? No way! There are now so many of us that you're no longer considered a weirdo who does strange things in private! These days, even most burger bars offer a meat-free alternative to minced cow.

A vegetarian is someone who doesn't eat any dead animals or bits taken from them. That means no meat; no poultry – chicken, turkey, etc; no fish or other water animals like prawns or crab; and no slaughter-house products such as gelatine and animal fat. A vegan is someone who doesn't eat any animal products at all, including eggs or dairy produce such as milk, cheese and butter.

Perhaps the most obscure-sounding of all the things to look out for and avoid is gelatine. In fact, it's in a lot of food that we generally don't think of as having anything to do with meat. Gelatine is a form of edible glue and is used to stick together sweets like some fruit gums, mints and licorice all-sorts. It's also used in some yoghurts and ice creams, as well as jellies.

Gelatine is made by boiling down the ligaments, tendons, bones, hooves and horns of pigs, cows and horses. In most European countries, manufacturers have to list all the ingredients of a product on the label so check on the packaging if you want to avoid gelatine. (As cows are used in the manufacture of gelatine, it's doubly important if you're worried about BSE.) You may find checking the labels a pain at first, but you soon get to know which products use gelatine and which don't. If you see the words 'guar gum' or 'agar agar' in the list of ingredients, don't worry. These are the veggie alternatives to gelatine, which more and more manufacturers are using instead.

Animal fat is just that – fat from the bodies of dead animals. It's boiled off the skin and used in some biscuits, margarine, cake, soups and other things. Suet is the fat taken from around an animal's kidneys. Fortunately, animal fat and suet are increasingly recognised as unhealthy, and loads of products now only use vegetable fats – again, just look at the list of ingredients on the package.

Label reading can be a drag as I've said, but there *are* ways of making it easier. Once you know a product is animal-free, you don't have to read the label again. There are also manufacturers who only produce vegetarian products, so once you discover who these are, you'll be able to buy their goods without worry. These brands are still mostly stocked by health-food shops but increasingly they're in a lot of supermarkets as well.

In fact, most of the foods we eat *don't* have bits of dead animal in them. Most kitchens usually have plenty to munch on which is veggie, including tins of beans, cereals, pasta and pasta dishes, vegetables, fruit, bread, veggie soups and veggie spreads, including yeast extracts like Marmite, Vegemite, Vecon and Promite, to name a few. So before your hunger pangs turn to panic, have a rake around in the cupboards at home and see what you find – you could be in for a pleasant surprise!

If you don't come up with much, it's time to visit the shops where you'll find a choice so wide you won't know where to start. Supermarkets, especially, have been quick to cash in on the growing veggie boom and nowadays sell most of the ingredients you'll need for a complete veggie meal.

Some supermarkets even have a 'special' vegetarian section, but this is really a bit pointless because vegetarian products are on virtually every shelf. In the tinned-food section, there is every imaginable fruit and vegetable. There are loads of pulses too – red kidney beans, black-eyed beans, canellini, borlotti beans and chick peas to name a few – all great for salads or to use instead of meat in casseroles, lasagne, bakes or pies. Tinned baked beans or curried baked beans, baked beans with veggie sausages in them, spaghetti hoops and vegetable bolognese in cans are also easy to find and cook. (Just pop them in a pot and heat them up.) There are plenty of tinned soups, too.

In the dried-foods section, you'll find all the different pastas as well as the jars of veggie sauces to go with them. Noodles are also good and easy to cook. There's every kind of rice, dried potatoes and even some products you may never have heard of before — bulgar wheat, cous cous and polenta. You can even get pizza bases in packs!

Now whizz your trolley round to the frozen-food cabinets and feast your eyes. Here are the veggie sausages, burgers and 'beef-like' pies, veggie-steaks and nuggets, imitation chicken and toad-in-the-hole, as well as ready-to-eat pasta dishes such as veggie lasagna and canneloni. The cooking instructions are dead simple. If the rest of your family is having meat and two veg, you can just heat up one of these to eat instead of the meat.

What often gives these frozen foods their 'meaty' feel is wheat protein (gluten) as well as textured vegetable protein (TVP) from soya beans. You can also buy TVP on its own as dried mince or in frozen chunks and make up your own dishes, using it in the same way you would meat to cook savoury 'mince', chilli, casseroles, shepherd's pie, curries and the like. If anyone asks, TVP is healthier than meat. It's high in protein and vitamins, and low in fat. (And no one's ever died from food poisoning or mad cow disease from eating TVP!)

As well as finding TVP sausages in the supermarket freezer, you'll probably find a whole range of non-meat bangers made from vegetables and tofu. Most of these taste spookily meaty. There's also a range of dry sausage mixes to which you add water, shape and then fry.

You can't get away from burgers even as a veggie, and again there are lots of different types. Some are made from chopped-up vegetables held together in a burger shape while others mimic meat. These days the veggie burger's in such big demand that most supermarkets have produced their own brands. I've even discovered a 'chargrilled burger' which I guarantee even the most blinkered carnivore couldn't tell from meat. (Once you become a more confident veggie cook, you may even want to make your own burgers with roast peanuts or TVP.)

Most of the big supermarkets also do their own range of ready-made vegetarian foods, from curries to mushroom stroganoff, cheese-and-spinach rolls to lasagne, cheese crowns to veggie cottage pies – all usually kept in the chiller cabinet. You don't have to be a whizz in the kitchen to get by. However, if you do want to get more involved in cooking, there are some good vegetarian cook books to help you get started, like *The L-Plate Vegetarian*, see page 189.

Be careful when buying cheeses because not all of them are vegetarian. To make a lot of cheeses, including Cheddar and Cheshire, a product called rennet is added to the milk to make it curdle. Most rennet comes from the stomachs of slaughtered calves but there is a vegetable variety and it's this that's used in veggie cheeses, including veggie Cheddar and Cheshire. So look for 'vegetarian cheese' or 'suitable for vegetarians' on the label. A lot of soft cheeses like Brie don't use rennet at all. However, if you're not sure or if the label isn't clear, don't be afraid to ask.

Ice creams too, believe it or not, aren't necessarily

vegetarian either. Pure dairy ice creams obviously are, but others are made from 'non-dairy' fat, which can either mean vegetable or animal fat, and it doesn't always say which on the label. Yes, you've guessed it — cold piggy cream in a tub!

There's often a big temptation when people first go veggie to overdose on cheese and other dairy products. Watch it! It isn't good to go overboard on these foods because at the end of the day you're still eating a type of animal fat.

If you've decided to skip all dairy products as well as meat, then the humble and amazingly versatile soya bean comes to the rescue again. Replace cow's milk with soya milk. It's available from almost all supermarkets and certainly all health-food shops. Different brands of soya milk taste very different from one another, so if you don't like one, try another. One of the most popular is the type that's sweetened slightly with apple juice and has calcium added to it. You can use it on your cereals, in tea, coffee and milk shakes, just as you would cow's milk.

I used to be a mega chocoholic and I still am! Only now I crave for plain, not milk, chocolate. Again there's a reasonable choice available in most shops and supermarkets but, until you learn which brands are milk-free and which aren't, you're probably better off in a health-food shop.

Cheese is usually the first thing people miss when they go vegan. However, you can buy some brilliant vegan cheeses, although they're not sold in supermarkets — yet. Ask your health-food shop to stock them if it doesn't have them already. One of the best is a soft cream cheese which tastes exactly as if it were made from cow's milk. You can even buy vegan hard cheeses, including Cheddar, Cheshire, Edam, Gouda, Mozzarella and even Stilton! For pizzas, try putting some extra tomato puree on the base and missing out on the cheese — it tastes great.

There are also several makes of vegan ice cream now available and although some are sold in supermarkets, the best place to look is still the health-food shop. Replacing butter on the other hand is dead easy as practically all the supermarkets sell an own-brand vegan margarine.

Basically, there are vegan alternatives for everything these days! (A brilliant book which lists them is the *Animal Free Shopper* by the Vegan Society — see p. 184.) Whatever it is you're looking for, the trick is not to rely just on the supermarket. Definitely check out your local health-food shop. It can be a bit daunting going in for the first time and you can feel embarassed because you don't recognise half the foods in the place! That was my experience, at any rate. But the staff are usually really helpful and if you can't find what you want, they often order it in.

There are now millions of young vegetarians in Britain and around the world. Despite this, there is a chance you may feel a bit isolated from your meat-eating friends to begin with. There may also be a whole host more questions you want to ask. If this is the case, then there are a number of veggie or environmental groups around which may be able to help you. Most of these are listed in the resource section at the back of this book — just get in touch with one that you think will be most useful to you. You don't necessarily have to become a member as most are happy to provide help and advice.

Never forget that you are a consumer and, as an individual, you have power. Don't be afraid to exercise it. You can choose what you do and don't buy, where you do and don't shop and which cafes you hang out in. We're always being told about choice, so where you have choice, use it!

If there are things that upset you, write to the organisations or people responsible. Don't be fobbed off. If you don't get the response you want, take it higher. If it's a company, writing to the managing director may be more successful than writing to a department manager. And bear in mind that acting with other people as a group will have added effect. So if you're complaining about a product, perhaps because it doesn't list its ingredients clearly, don't hesitate to let people know that you won't be buying it in future and that you'll also be telling all your friends to do the same.

By deciding to go veggie or vegan, you have changed your way of thinking. This simple fact will probably have an effect on lots of things – friends, the kinds of places you go and the things you do – you're unlikely to become a supporter of fox hunting for a start! You'll almost certainly get into debates, even arguments, and whether you realise it or not, you're going to start influencing other people simply by having made a stand on something important to you. That is one of the strongest things anyone can do! And you should feel proud!

As a virgin veggie, you've started down the road of change. The end may be a long way off, but we're getting there.

Chapter 19
Fancy Free and Cruelty Free

In becoming, being or staying veggie, you have taken one of the most important steps of your life. You've improved your health, made a giant contribution to improving people's lives around the world and done a huge amount to help the earth's environment. You've also made sure that the animal production line of misery and death is no longer carried out in your name. You are doing much more than most people to safeguard the future.

Of course, you're always going to meet those people who don't want to do anything. Once they know you're veggie, some bright wazzock is bound to tell you that, just by giving up meat and fish, you won't make any difference. Wrong! Just remember how many animals you will have saved in your lifetime by not eating meat: over 850 of them as well as half a ton of fish!

Having taken this important step, what sometimes happens is that people want to know more about the not-so-obvious and sometimes hidden cruelty to animals that plays a part in everyday life. This chapter outlines some additional issues that may concern you as a vegetarian or vegan, although you may feel quite fairly that you are doing enough already.

One obvious example of something that concerns a lot of veggies is the issue of leather. Leather is a by-product of meat. Producers don't kill cattle for their skin alone, although it is another bit of the animal that makes slaughtering them profitable for those who do it. Leather, as you probably know, has become pretty fashionable and is used for loads of things like shoes, briefcases and bags, as well as covering furniture.

A lot of the leather people buy is soft leather – the softer the better for handbags and jackets. This leather doesn't come from the skin of cows but from calves. And the softest leather of all comes from the unborn calf of a pregnant cow killed at the slaughterhouse. This leather is often used for gloves as well as clothes.

Happily, there are zillions of leather look-alike products these days. You can get bags and clothes from loads of shops and even by mail-order from specialist outlets (see pp. 184–5). There is also a wide range of non-leather jackets available and as a lot of them come from Italy – one of the international centres of fashion – they're really pretty up-to-date. They're also a lot cheaper than leather!

These days, non-leather shoes are easy to find too.

(It's a bit more difficult for boys although they are around.) You tend to get the best choice in cheaper shoe shops, funnily enough. The styles are the same as leather shoes it's just that they're less expensive. In the summer, hessian, canvas and rope shoes with synthetic soles tend to be everywhere. Again they're cheap and come in the latest styles.

If you're living in the UK, then Marks & Spencer (yes, really!) are stacked with pong-proof, non-leather boots and shoes and some are pretty cool. There are also specialist places whose whole purpose is to sell stylish veggie shoes by mail order (see p. 184). Most of these shops started up when the chunky Doc Marten look came in, and the stuff they sell is completely trendy. These shoes often aren't any cheaper than the leather styles, but you can even get identical DMs in brilliant colours like purple or yellow.

Wool is a bit like leather in that it often provides a bit of extra cash for sheep farmers. The reason some people don't use wool is because the shock of being shorn may kill some sheep while others sometimes die of cold if the shearing's done too early in the year while it's still winter. (What many people don't realise is that as much as 50 per cent of the wool used in brightly coloured coats, jumpers, scarves and gloves may be cut from the bodies of slaughtered sheep.) Happily, cotton has made a big hit over recent years and just about every jumper selection in shops, catalogues and mail-order stores includes a big range of cotton 'woollies'. Another alternative is acrylic and both this and cotton tend to be cheaper than wool, as well as a lot easier to look after and wash!

If you've decided not to use any animal products then fur's obviously a no-no too. Unless your folks have just won the lottery, you're unlikely to go clubbing in a mink or any other kind of fur – pardon the pun! Unfortunately, loads of shops still sell clothes with little bits of fur trim on the collars of jackets and coats. Fur can only come from one of two places: animals that have been trapped in the wild or those that have been farmed for their skin. Either way, the animals suffer and there are plenty of alternatives, including some really good fakes. Let's face it: Being a veggie and dressing in fur just don't go together!

Silk is seen as a trouble zone by some vegetarians and vegans. Silk is the substance that silk worms spin into a cocoon to protect themselves when they're in the process of turning from caterpillars into moths. Problem is, they never make it. While still in their cocoon, the caterpillars are dunked into boiling water which kills them and allows the silk to be unwound into a long thread. It's then woven into fabric to make the clothes you find in high-street stores everywhere.

Another slightly different issue that comes up for some vegetarians or vegans is dissection. If you're at school, then you may be asked to dissect an animal or part of it as part of your studies. However, in the UK, dissection is not required by the exam boards for GCSE Biology or for a teacher's assessment. So it doesn't *have* to be part of the lesson – it all depends on whether teachers (and students) want to include it or not. For this reason, schools in Britain cannot make their students take part in dissection and they can't take marks away from students who don't participate.

For some veggie students, dissection is no-go. As they see it, dissection teaches people to treat animals as disposable objects. Animals – usually rats, although in the USA, cats and piglets are also used – are bred, caged and killed just so they can be cut up in high-school science classes. The question is whether animals should be seen as teaching aids – or whether as living, feeling creatures, their lives have value in their own right.

Dissection is designed to show students how the structure of an animal's body is linked to its function. For instance, the position of the lungs has a bearing on how they work. Increasingly, however, exam boards have acknowledged that dissection is not essential to an understanding of this relationship. There are also a growing number of effective alternatives including computer simulations, videos and filmstrips, models, wall charts, prepared slides and, of course, diagrams in books – all of which give an equally good picture of how things work.

As we know, animals are also used to test how painful or dangerous different products like oven cleaners, bathroom cleaners, disinfectants, weed-killers and so on are when brought into contact with people's skin (including our nose, mouth and eyes). And, despite the growth of cruelty-free cosmetic companies, many big manufacturers still drip their make-up products into animals' eyes or smear them over their raw flesh, causing enormous pain and suffering.

Simply not buying cosmetics or domestic products that have been tested on animals sends a clear message to the manufacturers that you don't support what they are doing. As more people buy only 'cruelty-free' products, companies are turning away from animal testing in order to maintain sales.

The question is: How do you know which products are safe to buy? Well, you can be sure that none of the manufacturers who use animals is brave enough to tell you this by stamping 'Tested on animals' on their products. Instead, look out for the opposite. Read the labels and find out which companies have made a clear policy decision to give up animal testing. Then buy only from them. Most manufacturers who don't test on animals say so! To be a hundred per cent sure, you can also refer to the British Union for the Abolition of Vivisection's *Approved Product Guide* (see p. 181).

The more you change your life to cut out cruelty to animals, the more you may feel as though you're the only person in the world who cares. The truth is that a lot of people now care about the same things you do and are living accordingly – just see the number of different organisations listed at the end of this book!

On the other hand, you may feel that the number of issues to think about is a little overwhelming and that as a veggie, you're doing enough already. Giving up things like leather or wool may just seem too much at the moment. That's absolutely fine and it's important to remember that by being veggie, you are already doing much, much more than most.

Chapter 20
Keeping Cool at Home

Home is where the heart is. It can also be where the aggro is!

Some parents don't exactly jump up and down for joy when you tell them you're going veggie. Never mind, it isn't their fault. All they're guilty of is believing the myths about vegetarianism that most people are taken in by – you won't get enough protein, you'll fade away and die, you won't grow big and strong. Of course, none of this is true, so if you've got trouble at home like this, show them Section 3.

Parents who don't take this line often fall into a second category – the 'I'm not cooking two meals, I don't know what vegetarians eat, I haven't got time for these fads' category. Or it could just be that your parents don't want to face the fact that eating meat causes untold misery and suffering to animals so they make up all kinds of excuses about why they don't want you to change.

Perhaps the most difficult parent to persuade is the one who just insists point-blank that they're not going to let their daughter or son become vegetarian. This kind of response is most common from dads, and particularly the type of dad who has strong views on everything. He'll go purple in the face over 'mindless hooligans who care about nothing' but gets just as worked up over people who care about everything. You can't win, sometimes.

Fortunately, there's another type of parent and they're on the way to becoming the biggest group of all. These are the parents who are interested in what you're doing, why you're doing it and usually, after a few concerns about health, who will support you all the way.

Believe it or not, there are ways to deal with all the difficult types of parent successfully. The main thing is to avoid throwing a wobbler. The reason why parents object is largely ignorance. Most if not all parents genuinely believe what they're saying and care about your health and welfare — although sometimes, unfortunately, it is about control. What *you* have to do is stay calm and show them why they're wrong. Find out exactly what's worrying your parents, and then provide them with the information that answers their concerns.

Sally Dearing, 14, of Bristol told me, 'When I went veggie my mum went bananas. I was surprised at how strongly she reacted. I asked her what the problem was. Basically it came down to her knowing nothing about veggie nutrition or food. So I told her about all the diseases you can get from eating animals and how veggies get less heart disease and cancers. I just piled all the reasons on top of her and in the end she gave in! She bought some recipe books and I helped with the cooking. Anyway – guess what? After about two years she went veggie and even my dad has stopped eating red meat.'

Of course your parents might have an entirely different argument, claiming that animals are well cared for and humanely slaughtered so there's no need to worry. Again, show them the truth. What you mustn't expect is for them to change their opinion straight away. New information needs time to sink in – and folks generally have to swish it around their minds for a while and give it a bit of thought. What usually happens after a day or so is that parents think they've spotted a hole in your argument and can't wait to tell you why you're wrong. Listen to them, answer the argument, provide some more information and wait. They'll be back for more. This can go on for days, weeks or even months.

Parents often think that your vegetarianism is just a passing craze. The only way to prove to them that it isn't is to be firm about what you believe and stick to it. Believe me, it doesn't take long for them to take you seriously – if you are serious! I know, because I've been through it myself. I didn't handle it very well to begin with. I thought all I had to do was explain the truth about how animals were treated and my parents would change their whole lives immediately. They didn't – and instead of being patient I started raising my voice, blaming them, and telling them that *they* were responsible for animals' pain and suffering. Of course, they were responsible for some of it but that wasn't the best way to go about convincing them that my going veggie was grand.

In the end, my mum got pretty annoyed — maybe it was something to do with those 'Warning, this package contains a dead animal' stickers all over the kitchen?! But her irritation didn't last long. What she was guilty of was trying to sneak little bits of finely-chopped meat, usually chicken, into my meals because she thought I'd fade away without it. But I sussed out what was going on straight away and refused to eat the infected meals!

My mum stopped her sneaky tactics about a month later. Once it dawned on her that I had changed forever, we had long chats and she became very sympathetic — she even began cutting most meats out of her diet as well.

But what can you do with a stubborn parent who 'won't have this nonsense in my house?' If all the previous advice fails, then it depends on just how much aggro you're prepared to put up with. If you refuse to eat any meat or fish there is a good chance that he or she will change — in time. Basically, when they see you thrive on a veggie diet then at some point they will accept that it's a healthy way to live.

Some young people I know reach a compromise with their parents. Sometimes the offer comes from them because they can't stand the nagging any longer and sometimes it comes from the parents. It might be an agreement to eat fish but give up meat; or to eat free-range chicken and turkey but not red meat. For some people the compromise works; others find it unacceptable. Quite a few see it as a half victory and live with it – but only for the time being.

If you're faced with this situation, I can't tell you what to do. You might want to treat a compromise as a step forward or you might feel you have to stick to your principles. You might decide to wait until you're more in control of your own life before becoming vegetarian. It's difficult, particularly if you know the objections are unfounded, like when your parents insist that vegetarianism is unhealthy. In the end, only you can decide.

Leanne McCrorie, 15, from Glasgow, found her dad to be a problem when she went veggie. She says, 'My dad tried to make me eat meat again – it was like he didn't want to be proved wrong and took it as some kind of personal insult that I didn't want to be like him.' But in time she was pleasantly surprised at what happened. 'Mum and dad started to eat veggie food with me and now say that they really like it!'

What can be really irritating is when parents or grandparents blame your vegetarianism for everything that goes wrong in your life! Judith Rushman, 15, of North London experienced this: 'If I got a cold my nan would say "See, I knew it – it's that diet of yours." My mum even brought up vegetarianism when I fractured my ankle at school!' Still, the truth will out! Judith's family are 'much more understanding. It's taken three years, but my mum actually thinks that meat's unhealthy now.'

What can sometimes help with any parental ruck is to get another adult to argue your case for you. If you know an adult veggie make sure they know exactly how you feel and get them to talk to your parents on your behalf.

It's likely that most of the objections you face are really more to do with 'inconvenience' than anything else. Offer to help with the shopping and cooking so your mum or dad isn't left scratching her or his head not knowing what to buy or cook. Even better, cook a meal for the whole family at least once a week. Help them by finding out the kind of foods that are quick and simple to prepare and cook.

Fortunately, most people have a lot more knowledge about vegetarianism than they did a few years ago and many parents are pleased when their kids go veggie. If it was that difficult there wouldn't be half a million teenage veggies in Britain alone.

'I'm a vegetarian because I can't stand the horrific way animals are killed just for food. If your parents are difficult, just state why you are vegetarian and prepare to be flexible – don't alienate yourself. Try helping with some meals. In the end they'll realise that vegetarianism saves animals and the environment and that it's the right thing to do!'

Damon Albarn, lead singer of Blur

Pointers to Dealing with Parents

You have to be reasonable with parents – to a degree!
The trouble is, left alone they may make the wrong decisions.
So, be clear where you can have influence.
Help with the shopping and, at the same time, try to make sure your
folks don't buy battery eggs or veal etc.
If they don't agree you could:

- **Reason with them. Explain calmly how battery hens/veal calves are treated and show them lots of pictures which you can get from animal rights organisations like Viva! Explain to your mum and dad that they're responsible for animal suffering if they keep buying these products.**

- **If the supermarket charges a fortune for free-range eggs, shop around. Health-food shops, markets and farms usually sell them much cheaper.**

- **Really shock your parents and offer to do the washing up for a week if they buy free-range eggs/don't eat veal/ eat more veggie food.**

If that doesn't work, you could be less subtle and:

- **Accidently drop all the battery eggs on the kitchen floor. Then point out that the eggs break more easily because the shells are thin due to the poor condition of the birds.**

- **If meat is the offending item, forget to put it away; leave it close to the cat's dish instead.**

- **Paint or felt-tip the eggs with sad faces of hens and messages like 'Warning – Salmonella' and 'Laid in Pain'.**

- **Sneakily swap the battery eggs for free-range eggs in the shopping trolley when no one's looking.**

- **Get loads of great veggie recipes and – eek – help with the cooking.**

Chapter 21
Standing Up for Yourself at School

Young people have rights! According to the organisation the United Nations, you have the right to be educated, eat healthy food and get decent health care. You also have a right to life – which is the basic right not to be killed. When you look across the world at the fighting and destruction taking place, you might wonder sometimes what's happened to those rights.

In the West, young people have other rights that we tend to take for granted. At school, no one expects a Muslim or Catholic to attend a Protestant church service. If you're Jewish, you have the right not to be served pork in your school dinner; and if you're Catholic, you don't expect to be served fish on Fridays. These are religious rights but there are others, too, such as the right of a pacifist not to be forced into the army. It's all about conscience – not doing something which offends your personal beliefs. Everyone should have that right whatever their age.

However, you may find you are unhappy about something which clashes with your beliefs at school – and I don't mean a belief in not doing homework! It has to be something which really offends your conscience. It could be that you're asked to do something which you believe is racist or sexist. Or it could be something which is in conflict with your belief in the rights of animals not to suffer. Whatever it is, you have a right not to participate in that activity because it goes against your beliefs. But you have to plan how you're going to do it.

One issue which may arise, for example, is the question of dissection. It may be that you find dissection objectionable but that your school expects you to take part.

The first thing to do is to ask at the beginning of the school year whether dissection is going to be included in your science or biology class. If this is the case, the next step is to gather as much information as possible about the subject – the alternatives to dissection, the school's policy, and whether the school is legally entitled to make you take part. The best way of doing this is to make contact with national or local organisations which will support you and give you the latest information (see the index of organisations on pp. 180–83.)

In the UK, you don't have to take part in dissection. Teachers can't make you nor can they mark you down for refusing. (Of course, some may not tell you this!) You may find, however, that your school has a policy of exempting veggie students from dissection. The thing to do is to plan what you're going to say, then go and see your teacher. Explain your objections and ask to be given an alternative. Stay calm and be polite. The worst thing you can do is get drawn into a shouting match. If you find it hard to talk to your teacher, write a letter instead. You may also want to ask your parents to write a letter supporting your choice. (Although you don't need your parent's support to act on and defend your beliefs, it can help!)

Many teachers are understanding, particularly if you give them a chance to make alternative arrangements, rather than just opting out on the day of the dissection. However, some teachers aren't so helpful and might refuse to do anything. In this case, you may want to consider organising further support.

Jennifer Neal is a sixth-form student. She was asked to dissect a rat when she was 15, and she says:

The rats were stiff, so to open them out flat on their backs to cut open their stomachs, their legs had to be broken and pins put through their paws. The teacher told us not to think of it as breaking bones, but to imagine we were breaking bits of plastic.

I refused to take part and my teacher made fun of me. The next day I wrote to Animal Aid for leaflets and petitions against dissection and gave them out to my class. I was surprised at how many people agreed with me, even though they'd gone ahead and done the dissection! Most of my class signed the petition and so we had a meeting to decide what to do next.

About ten of us gave out more petitions to other years in the school and we collected signatures in our breaks. In the end about three-quarters of the school signed. We then arranged a meeting with the head of biology and handed the signatures to him. We also took along a booklet of alternatives to dissection and asked for them always to be available.

At first he tried to make us out to be trouble makers, but I think our strength of numbers really made a difference because after a while he listened to us. A week later, he said in class that the school was going to buy alternatives for anyone who didn't want to dissect. Most people chose the alternatives and eventually, the school phased out dissection altogether.

All this isn't just theory, it works. Students all over countries such as Britain and New Zealand have brought an end to dissection in their schools.

Another big issue you may be faced with at school is the right to veggie meals. Some schools have moved with the times and provide pretty delish veggie food every day, but if your's isn't one of them, don't be afraid to ask for a better choice. Again gather together as much information as you can: about what other schools in your area offer, what groups such as the World Health Organisation think about a veggie diet and, of course, use the information in this book. Start by keeping a note of what veggie food is offered over the course of a week or more in your school.

When politicians want to change things they usually try to find out how much support they've got. You can do the same. You could do a survey of other pupils to see what they want, find out the teachers' views and perhaps even a few parents. See how many would like a decent veggie option every day – it probably won't be just veggies who support you either, many meaties also like to have the choice.

Finally, arm yourself with recipes which are suitable

for school caterers and then go and see your head teacher or cook. Most respond well (honest!) and will add at least one proper veggie meal a day. If you're unlucky and come up against the 'I can't be doing with these fads' type of attitude there are other things you can do.

Parents can play an important part so try to get them involved. If they're sympathetic, ask your mum or dad to have a little word in the head teacher's lug hole; this usually works wonders! The more parents and teachers who are involved the better. Again, get as many pupils involved as possible and get a petition going. It's your right to be vegetarian and most schools do accept their responsibility to cater for you – but if they don't, sort 'em out!

Graeme Simmons, 16, of Brighton definitely needed a campaign for better veggie meals at his school. He explains:

When I went veggie I asked the cook what food I could eat. She gave me a bowl of pea and ham soup and told me to take out the meat! I couldn't get through to her, so I went to see the head teacher. She was quite sympathetic and admitted some teachers wanted veggie food as well. She had a meeting with the caterers that provided food to the school and we were given a choice of one main vegetarian meal a day after that. It's not great but it's better than being offered dead pig!

Laura Jones, 14, of Oswestry in Shropshire has gone a step further. Her school provides vegetarian and vegan options daily:

I contacted the veggie organisation Viva! for recipes and had a meeting with the head cook. I couldn't believe how helpful she was, she saw vegan cooking as a new challenge and her food is amazing. The only problem is that the meat eaters all now want the veggie choices so I have to get to the counter before it's all gone!

Unfortunately, not all schools are open minded. Katherine Leaf, 15, of Glasgow says that her school is:

embarrassingly backward when it comes to vegetarianism. There are three veggies in my class but other pupils and teachers weren't interested when we tried to get a veggie option on the menu. Even my mum contacted the head teacher, but suddenly I went from being seen as just normal Kathy to a stirrer and then my friends backed out of the campaign. They said it was because they'd decided to take packed lunches, but really they were scared of getting into trouble! I still can't believe that the head teacher takes vegetarianism as some kind of personal threat!

When you plan a campaign, first be aware of the kind of influences schools are under. They are usually under huge pressure from governments who provide the money out of people's taxes to pay teachers' wages and run the schools. It is often governments who set the curriculum, decide class sizes and even dictate the content of lessons. In the end, teachers have to answer to government for the money they spend and the decisions they make. If things aren't seen as going well in schools it's generally the teachers who are blamed.

When you try to make demands at school you are, in a way, challenging teachers' judgement and control.

Some teachers and school authorities may react by thinking, 'If it's any good for them, we would have thought of it already!' Teachers are themselves usually under a lot of pressure from those above them and they might not have the energy – or inclination to deal with pressure from you, too. Many won't react like this, but be prepared for the worst. If you want to be taken seriously then you have to prove to the teachers that you are for real.

The first and most important lesson, as I've said before, is to gather the facts. The second is that there's strength in numbers. It doesn't really matter what you're complaining about – dissection, school meals, better resources – you should tackle them all in much the same way. Argue your case amongst your friends and class-mates everywhere you can get them to listen. Gather like-minded people around you and work out exactly what it is you're complaining about and what action you want the school to take. If you don't make clear and easily understood requests, the chances are that nothing will happen.

Sometimes the biggest problem in organising support is apathy – other pupils just can't be bothered. This might be because they don't share your concern, because they don't know the truth of the situation or because it's the type of school that squashes any initiatives. Sometimes students think they're powerless and can't change anything.

The answer to apathy is information and involvement. Make sure people know all the information you have available and try getting them actively working on something. You might do it by forming small groups with special tasks, perhaps to find out what other schools in the area are doing on your particular issue or what help different pressure groups and charities can offer.

At the end of the day, you might find that the issue which concerns you isn't of any interest to other pupils. If that is the case you can carry on by yourself but it might make success a bit harder to achieve.

If you are working with others, it's important to be democratic and to listen to all viewpoints. Don't allow one person to dominate the meetings or to belittle others in the group. Encourage everyone to have a say. But you can't debate things indefinitely and there comes a time when you have to take decisions. Again, do it democratically and having reached a decision – stick to it. If you ignore the majority view the group is likely to fall apart.

You also need to be prepared for some of your supporters to cave in and desert you at the first bit of conflict. Now that you know this may happen, try and prepare for it. Decide between you what it is you're prepared to settle for and how far everyone is prepared to go to get it. Once everyone's had their say, they all understand what's involved, and you've made the decision, tell the group that anyone who is not prepared to go along with the decision should leave now. Really stress it. They probably won't leave, and it will make it more difficult for them to back out later.

Once you've decided to do something – do it! If you don't act your supporters will lose interest. Even if your first demand is just a verbal request to a teacher, tackle it seriously. Plan what you want to say, make a note of the main points so you don't forget them and work out in your head the words you intend to use. You may find it helps to practise saying them out loud so you feel confident about them in your meeting.

When the meeting's over, make a note of the date and time, who you spoke to, what decision was reached and why. You need these details to remind you of what happened when you report back to the group, even more importantly, you might also need to refer back to them one day in order to prove a point about what was said or agreed.

If this first meeting is unsuccessful, put your request in writing and send it to someone more senior. Be polite and calm, avoid using aggressive or confrontational language, set out your demands clearly – the reasons for them and what you want to happen. Obviously, the furthest you can go in the school itself is the principal or head teacher. If you have to take it that far, use every means possible to spread news of your request to other students. Put notices up on your school bulletin board, write in to the school magazine, raise it with the school council if there is one, and gather as much support around you as you possibly can.

If you don't get any joy from the head teacher, you can take your request even further: to the Board of Governors, for instance, or the Parent Teacher Association (PTA). Each time you go a step further, include details of the previous steps in your request – what was said and what has been decided so far.

More often than not, the situation will have been resolved or a compromise reached before this stage.

However, if your request still isn't being taken on board, there is still more you can do. If you genuinely feel your grievance is real and isn't being taken seriously, you can try getting support further afield. One way of doing this is by getting publicity in the local press, including newspapers, radio and television. But be very careful before you do this. Once you start down this road you are in much deeper water. You need to be very sure it is the issues which are important to you and not the glory. You will also need a lot of support because once you take this step, it becomes very hard for the school, the Board of Governors, or anyone else, to back down. The only way of settling this situation is by compromise – each side giving in on something. So again, you need to ask yourself what it is you're prepared to compromise on.

If you do decide to go ahead with this step, then the 'Letters to the Editor' section is a good place to start. This is because letters tend not to be interfered with and are printed as you wrote them. If a journalist decides to interview you, that's a different matter. It could be exactly the break you need, but be careful. Media often has its own agenda and journalists may decide that the real story isn't the one you want them to cover.

For them it might be much more interesting to do a piece about bolshy school kids challenging their 'elders and betters'. You know the kind of thing – 'Bring back the cane! It wasn't like this in my day! It's all the fault of pop groups/drink/teenage sex! What's happening to the world?' If that *does* happen then you'll know you've got right up their nose – and probably have a very good case!

However great the uproar and however far you go, the most important thing is never to lose sight of what you're arguing for. Most people respect beliefs, principles and courage; hardly anyone respects a loud mouth!

Asking for change means questioning the powers that be, and won't always be welcome. Every veggie, often without realising it, is doing this to some degree. But even if you don't win a particular campaign, you will have influenced others. Simply by stating your beliefs, you will have planted a seed in other people's minds which may affect their attitude in the future . . . to animals and perhaps to a lot of things. So don't be afraid to make your voice and views heard.

Chapter 22
Friends and Foe

'It's funny, but when I went veggie I was worried about what my friends would think.' If that's how you feel, then you're probably in for a nice surprise. Most young people can see that going veggie is a positive step that saves animals. This doesn't mean that they'll all want to join you, but at least some of them will already be heading in the same direction! Georgina Harris, 15, of Manchester remembers, 'All my friends thought going veggie was really cool. And lots of people would say "Oh yeah, I'm a veggie too" even if they weren't!'

Of course, you're bound to come across some drongo who'll make pathetic attempts at teasing you for your beliefs. 'Rabbit food — that's all she eats'; 'Aaah, here comes the little bunny lover' are about as intelligent as the comments get. Often the reason they do it is because you show them up. It takes courage to be different and you're showing these people that you're strong and they're not – and that worries them.

Be prepared for the macho rubbish. Leanne Smith, 16, got really fed up with a friend of her father's.

He was always having a go at me about being too emotional and not living in the real world. He used to call it teasing and although he had a smile on his face when he did it I know it wasn't meant to be funny – it was spiteful. He was trying to make out that because I was female I was weak or something.

He used to go shooting a lot and one Sunday afternoon he called in to see dad and just threw a dead rabbit down on the kitchen table in front of me, laughing. 'There's a nice little furry bunny for you', he said. I was so disgusted that for the first time I told him, in no uncertain terms, what I thought of him but without being hysterical. I think he was shocked. Certainly my dad was and I don't think he's seen the bloke since.

There's a lesson in Leanne's story. Whatever you do, keep cool! It's only fun taking the Mickey if you get a reaction. It won't take long before everyone gets used to you being veggie, then the jokes become boring and stop.

The biggest reaction you're likely to get is one of genuine interest. The number of veggies in Britain and many other countries is sky-rocketing, so be ready for questions such as, 'What do you eat?'. Joanna Bates, 12, of Northampton says 'At first my friends kept asking me if I missed meat – until they decided they preferred my food to their own. Also they started to associate meat with a dead animal and in the end four out of five have also become vegetarian.'

Some would-be veggies give up because all their mates want to meet at the local burger bar. That used to be a problem once when there was no veggie alternative and even the chips were cooked in beef fat. It shows just how strong veggie pressure is getting because most of the big burger chains now sell veggie burgers and cook their chips in vegetable oil.

Being invited round to friends' houses isn't the problem you'd think. Once people know you're a veggie most parents make an effort. You can help them out by giving a simple suggestion – like popping a veggie 'meat' pie in the oven with their food and sharing the veg. If you do finish up with veg alone it's not a major problem; you're not going to die.

Friends sometimes – and enemies always – try to pick holes in your beliefs. The funny thing is, everyone thinks they've come up with a totally original jibe. 'I bet you'd eat an animal if you were stranded on a desert island and that's all there was!' The answer – 'Yeah, I probably would, but then I'd probably eat you if you were there' – may not have much to do with modern meat production but then neither does the question.

From years of experience, I've put together a list of the most common and most irritating questions you're ever likely to be asked (see pp. 173–7). If this, and all else fails, then just tell them to bog off!

Now for the mega question. Do you snog a meat eater? If you don't, you might find your choice a bit limited. On the other hand, the veggie perfect person might be just around the corner or at the next club you go to. If you want to meet a veggie male then go where veggie males are more likely to be – local vegetarian, environmental or animal rights groups – and give the rugby-club dance a miss. If you want to meet a veggie female the same kind of rules apply – the only difference is, it's much easier because there are twice as many veggie females as males.

On the other hand, you could decide to snog meat eaters but convert them. Use all the same techniques as used for parents – videos showing how animals live and die are a must, and you can borrow them from most animal rights or veggie groups. Be strong and insist you only go to those places where you have a choice of things to eat. And it's perfectly fair to want to go to purely vegetarian places some of the time – maybe even half of the time because your views count as much as theirs.

If partners refuse to budge from their meaty ways, even after you've tried everything, then you have a problem and a difficult decision to make. Do you ignore it or give them the elbow? On the other hand, if they respect your views enough to at least eat veggie when they're with you, you could be on to a winner.

I've met some veggies who won't even talk to meat eaters if they can avoid it. You're certainly not going to convert anyone to veggiedom that way! And more than one person has converted their partner – I know, I speak from experience!

'You don't have to kill to live life to the full. If you or your mates want to go veggie, take it from me it's a lot easier than you think and a great way to live. And anyway, vegetarians make better snoggers...'

Margi Clarke, actress

Answers to the Most Irritating Questions You're Bound to be Asked

The moment some people know you're a veggie, they're likely to ask a question or have a dig which they think is not only brilliant and original but will completely burst your veggie balloon. I've heard them all before – so here are a few suggestions for demolishing those pesky know-it-alls!

If everyone goes veggie, what'll happen to all the animals – we'll be over-run?

Oh sure! Like all these caged pigs and chickens are having a great time having sex all day long – not! Farmers control how many animals are born – if you don't eat 'em, they don't breed 'em.

173

Then what will happen?
All the animals will die out.

Of course! There were no animals at all on the earth before humans came along. Now why didn't I realise that?

How do you know vegetables don't feel pain?

(You know you're winning the argument when you hear this one!)

If you see a cabbage screaming its head off and running down the high street, call me. We'll be witnessing the first ever veg with a central nervous system.

But I've heard that plants scream when they're cut.

No they don't – not even when watching Hammer House of Horror movies. The sounds picked up by electronic equipment when plants are cut are thought to be made by gases. The cut releases pressure inside the plant, causing gases to move towards the opening, making a noise as they go.

It's natural to eat meat – we're meant to eat it!

If you ate nothing but meat and dairy products you'd die within a year. The average life expectancy for a vegan or veggie is in the 80s. On the other hand, may be it *is* natural for drongos to die young – natural selection anyway.

But meat's full of protein that helps build muscle.

Yeah, which is why a gorilla – which eats nothing but veg – is so big and strong.

Vegetarians eat chicken, don't they?

No they don't! What do you think a chicken is, second cousin to a carrot? And just for the record, vegetarians don't eat humans either, no matter how thick they are.

(The same answer can apply to questions about fish or seafood. Or ask the questioner when the last time was that they grew mackerel at the bottom of their garden.)

You're only one person,
so what difference does it make?

Oh, I'm only saving the lives of 5 cows, 20 pigs, 29 sheep, 760 chickens, 46 turkeys, 15 ducks, 7 rabbits and half a ton of fish. What are you doing?

If we all went vegetarian, there wouldn't be
enough land to grow all the food we need.

Who do you think eats more cereal in a day, you or a cow? If we all went veggie, we'd need half the land used now. If we all went vegan, we'd need less than a quarter.

What's the point of being vegetarian
if you wear leather?

Being a veggie still saves hundreds more animals than being a meatie, no matter what you wear!

Why do vegetarians always
look so unhealthy?

So Madonna, Damon Albarn, Heather Small, Jason Orange, kd lang and Carl Lewis all look like they're at death's door, do they?

It's veggies who are putting
farmers out of work.

It's not. Growing plant foods needs more labour, so the more veggies there are, the more work there'd be on farms. Meat is now a mechanised industry that's putting people out of work.

If animals weren't happy,
they wouldn't put on weight.

So if I chained you to the floor in a tiny concrete cell, where there was nothing to look at or do except eat, you'd lose weight?

Chickens wouldn't lay eggs if they were unhappy.

That's like saying that you'd stop going to the loo if you felt hacked off.

How do you know animals are unhappy or don't like the way they're treated?

How do you know when you've been run over by a bus? Maybe you'd skip into a slaughterhouse singing 'kill me, kill me'. Most animals have more sense.

But animals don't complain.

No, animals don't talk – unlike some people who go on and on. Loads of studies have been done and surprise, surprise, they all show that most farm animals are in pain. You'd never have known that without going to university, would you?

What do you eat instead of meat?

Pizza, sausages, chilli, shepherds' pie, curry, burgers, hot dogs, lasagne, pies, flans, cannelloni, spaghetti, nuggets . . . continue until out of breath . . .
(Alternatively, if you want to save your breath, ask the questioner what they eat and then you can just say 'So do I' because there's a veggie alternative to most things these days!)

But veggie food is boring.

(Yawn, yawn.) Well, maybe if you're in the kitchen. We all know a meal is as interesting as the cook who makes it.

You've got your priorities wrong. You care more about animals than people.

(This is always said by people who aren't doing anything to help anyone.)
Eating meat is all about taking food from the poor to feed to the rich. By being veggie, I'm not just helping animals but the world and all the people on it. I'm happy to make an exception though in your case!

It's okay for adults to be veggie, but not kids.
Yeah, it's only reasonable that kids get their fair share of
heart disease and cancer. After all, only the USA government
and British Medical Association reckon that sprog vegetarians
have excellent health.

There goes the bunny—lover.
Hooray, another witty comment from Mr Salami Skin!

**Why don't you have just a small piece of meat?
I won't tell!**
And I won't tell anyone how stupid you are. Read my lips:

I love
being a
vegetarian!

(And I hope you do too!)

A Last Word!

So you're a veggie or vegan – or about to become one! Is that the end of the story? Well, it needn't be. What you're doing is great and it means that no animal will ever again be killed for you. But I hope this book has also shown you that you can stand up for what you believe in and make a difference in this world.

When you boil it down, the excuses people give for eating meat are just that – excuses. They say it's natural – but we know it's not. They say animals are well cared for and killed humanely – we know that's untrue. They claim we need meat for good health – when the opposite is true. They even make out that the trade in meat helps the poorer parts of the world – when in fact it destroys them. (We've also seen what it does to the planet!) I've tried to explain why people are encouraged to think like this.

The most important thing is that by going veggie you are taking a huge step towards changing things for the better. By giving up meat, fish and slaughterhouse products, you're saying to the world that you care about the future. Because you're a veggie, animals will no longer suffer on your behalf. You are saying no to starvation and helping the environment. You are caring for your own health – and taking responsibility for what you believe.

Above all, you can be proud because you are doing so much when a lot of people are still doing so little. And they will learn by your example. Well done!

Addresses of Organisations

Here's a list of useful contacts who will be pleased to provide you with information. Call or write — a self addressed envelope is appreciated.

Organisations — UK

Advocates for Animals, 10 Queensferry Street, Edinburgh EH2 4PG. Tel 0131 225 6039. Animal protection group against all animal abuse.

Animal Aid, The Old Chapel, Bradford Street, Tonbridge, Kent TN9 1AW. Tel 01732 364546. Concerned with all aspects of animal abuse, it has a youth section and local groups across the UK.

Animal Concern, Tel 0141 445 3570. Campaigns on all areas of animal cruelty.

Beauty Without Cruelty Charity, 57 King Henry's Walk, London N1 4NH. Tel 01983 731491 Campaigns to end the slaughter of animals in the name of beauty and fashion.

Born Free Foundation, Cherry Tree Cottage, Cold-harbour, Dorking, Surrey RH5 6HA. Tel 01306 712091. Against circuses, zoos and run the EleFriends campaign.

British Union for the Abolition of Vivisection (BUAV), 16a Crane Grove, London N7 8LB. Tel 0171 700 4888. Campaigns to abolish experiments on animals.

Compassion in World Farming (CIWF), 5a Charles Street, Petersfield, Hants GU32 2EH. Tel 01730 264208. Campaigns against farm animal cruelty. Has local groups throughout Britain.

Dr Hadwen Trust for Humane Research, 22 Bancroft, Hitchin, Herts SG5 1JW. Tel 01462 436819. Information on, or funding for, alternatives to experiments on animals.

Environmental Investigation Agency, Tel 0171 490 7040. Campaigns to save wild animals.

Farm Animal Welfare Network, PO Box 40 Holmfirth, Huddersfield HD7 1QY. Tel 01484 688650. Incorporates Chickens Lib with masses of info on poultry farming.

Friends of the Earth, 26–28 Underwood Street, London N1 7JQ. Tel 0171 490 1555 Campaigns on a whole range of environmental issues including rainforest destruction and pollution through pesticides.

Greenpeace, Canonbury Villas, London N1 2PN. Tel 0171 354 5100. Campaigns on a wide range of environmental issues.

Humane Research Trust, 29 Bramhall Lane South, Bramhall, Cheshire SK7 2DN. Tel 0161 439 8041. Information on and funding for research into human illness using non-animal techniques.

Hunt Saboteurs Youth Group, Animal Freedom, PO Box 127, Kidderminster, Worcs DY10 3UZ. Tel 01562 700086. Against all blood sports.

International Fund for Animal Welfare (IFAW), Warren Court, Park Road, Crowborough, E Sussex TN6 2GA. Tel 01892 663819. General animal welfare group.

Jewish Vegetarian Society, 855 Finchley Road, London NW11 8LX. Tel 0181 455 0692. Information on all aspects of going vegetarian.

League Against Cruel Sports (LACS), 83–87 Union Street, London SE1 1SG. Tel 0171 407 0979. Campaigns against blood sports.

People for the Ethical Treatment of Animals (PETA), PO Box 3169, London SW15 3ZG. Tel 0181 785 3113. Campaigns against all animal abuse.

Pisces, BM Fish, London WC1N 3XX. Tel 0171 278 3068 Campaigns against angling.

Respect for Animals, PO Box 500, Nottingham NG1 3AS. Tel 0115 952 5440. Campaigns against fur and live exports.

RSPCA, Causeway, Horsham, West Sussex RH12 1HG. Tel 01403 264181. Promotes animal welfare.

Vegan Society, 7 Battle Road, St Leonards on Sea, E Sussex TN27 7AA. Tel 01424 427393. Information on all aspects of veganism.

Viva!, 12 Queen Square, Brighton BN1 3FD. Tel 01273 777688. Viva! (Vegetarians International Voice for Animals) was launched by the author of this book in 1994. It is a vegetarian and vegan charity with a special section for under 18s. It produces loads of free info to help you change your diet and campaigns on issues such as factory farming, slaughter and live exports. Viva! also has free packs on campaigning for veggie school meals, how to Convert-a-Parent and SCOFF! (Schools' Campaign Opposed to Factory Farming).

World Society for the Protection of Animals, 2 Langley Lane, London SW8 1TJ. Tel 0171 793 0540. International group for animal welfare.

World-Wide Fund for Nature, Panda House, Weyside Park, Godalming, Surrey GU7 1XR. Tel 01483 426444 Campaigns for wildlife conservation.

Organisations – USA

American Vegan Society, Box H, 501 Old Harding Highway, Malaga, California, CA 08328. Tel 609 694 2887. Great information base for vegans.

Animal Welfare Institute, PO Box 3650, Washington DC 20007. Tel 202 337 2332. International organisation publicising animal issues of all kinds, including factory farming, anti-vivisection, anti-whaling and the plight of exotic birds in the pet trade.

Earthsave International, 620 B Distillery Commons, Louisville KY 40206. Tel 408 423 4069. Campaigning group with info on how meat eating destroys the planet.

Farm Sanctuary, PO Box 150, Watkins Glen NY 14891. Tel 607 583 2223. Sanctuary for rescued farm animals. Also campaigns against the abuse of farm animals.

Humane Farming Association, PO Box 3577, San Rafael CA 94912. Tel 415 485 1495. Campaigns against factory farming.

In Defense of Animals, 131 Camino Alto, Mill Valley CA 94941. Tel: 415 388 9641. Dynamic animal rights group – fighting against the fur and meat trades, captive whales, vivisection and more.

People for the Ethical Treatment of Animals, (PETA), 501 Front Street, Norfolk VA 23510. Tel 757

622 7382. www.peta-online.org The USA's largest animal protection group actively campaigns against all animal abuse, with many successes. PETA has an education department which is working to stop dissection and has lots of free youth materials covering everything from the meat and fur trades to anti-vivisection and performing animals. And PETA's brilliant magazine, *Animal Times*, is not to be missed!

Physicians Committee for Responsible Medicine, 5100 Wisconsin Avenue NW, Suite 404, Washington DC 20016. Tel 202 686 2210. Produces excellent info on why a vegan diet is the healthiest on Earth! And it's all written by top doctors.

United Poultry Concerns, PO Box 59367, Potomac MD 20859. Tel 301 948 2406. Uncovers the truth behind the poultry industry with great campaigns and information.

Vegan Action, PO Box 4353, Berkley, California CA 94704. Tel 510 843 6343. Educational group promoting veganism, with plenty of materials on animals, the environment and health. Also produce a monthly newsletter.

Vegan Outreach, 10410 Forbes Road, Pittsburgh, Pennsylvania PA 15235. Tel 412 968 0268. Educational group who produce the popular pamphlet for college students 'Why Vegan'. Provides information on factory farming, slaughter, health and help for people wanting to change their diet.

Vegetarian Resource Group, PO Box 1463, Baltimore MD 21203. Tel 410 366 8343. www.vrg.org Contact for plenty of info on anything and everything vegetarian. Produce a guide to vegetarian restaurants in the USA.

Vivavegie Society, PO Box 294, Prince Street Station, New York NY 10012. Tel 212 966 2060. Active campaigning group on all the veggie issues. Encourages voluntary help.

World Society for the Protection of Animals, PO Box 190, 29 Perkins Street, Boston, Massachusetts MA 02130. Tel 617 522 7000. International campaigns on a wide range of animal welfare issues.

Youth for Environmental Sanity (YES), 420 Bronco Road, Soquel CA 95073. Tel 408 662 0793. Inspires young people to take positive action for the planet. Runs one and two week long camps to educate youth as the support and voice for the youth environmental movement.

Organisations – Australia

All Animal Liberation groups actively campaign against all animal abuse including dissection and factory farming. They encourage teenagers to help out as volunteers.
Animal Liberation (ACT), PO Box 1875, Canberra ACT 2601. Tel 02 6247 4358.
Animal Liberation (Newcastle), PO Box 136, Newcastle NSW 2300. Tel 0249 524 121.
Animal Liberation (NSW), Suite 509, 410 Elizabeth

186

Street, Sydney NSW 2000. Tel 02 9212 6253.

Animal Liberation (QLD), 131 Melbourne Street, South Brisbane QLD 4101. Tel 07 3844 5533.

Animal Liberation (SA), PO Box 114, Rundle Mall, Adelaide SA 5000. Tel 08 8231 8785.

Animal Liberation (Tas) Inc, Environment Centre, 102 Bahurst Street, Hobart TAS 7000. Tel 002 287 071.

Animal Liberation (Vic), PO Box 12838, A'Beckett Street, Melbourne VIC 3000. Tel 03 9419 5188.

Animal Liberation (WA), PO Box 8173, Perth WA 6849.

Animal Watch Australia, PO Box 1630, Collingwood VIC 3066. Tel 03 9415 1797. Concerned with all aspects of animal cruelty.

Animals Australia, PO Box 1023, Collingwood VIC 3066. Tel 03 9415 1797. Provide free information on all aspects of animal abuse; acts as an umbrella group for all animal organisations.

Australian Wildlife Protection Council, 1st floor, 247 Flinders Lane, Melbourne VIC 3000. Tel 03 9650 8326. Active campaigns to save the kangaroo and other wildlife.

International Fund for Animal Welfare, PO Box 322, Helensburgh NSW 2508. Tel 0242 942 222. Campaigns against all animal abuse.

People Against Cruelty in Animal Transport (PACAT), PO Box 152, Sth Fremantle WA 6162. Tel 08 9377 0781. Active group which works to ban live exports.

Vegetarian and vegan organisations produce information on all the main issues and will help you change your diet.

Vegan Society (NSW), PO Box 467, Broadway NSW 2007. Tel 02 4721 5068.

Vegan Society of WA, PO Box 8173, Perth WA 6849.

Vegetarian Society (NSW) Inc, PO Box 65, Paddington NSW 2021. Tel 02 9698 4339.

Vegetarian Society of Victoria, PO Box 1228, Collingwood VIC 3066. Tel 03 9415 7166.

Vegetarian Society of WA, PO Box 220, North Perth WA 6006.

Vegetarian/Vegan Society of Queensland, 1086 Waterworks Road, The Gap QLD 4061. Tel 07 3300 9320.

Organisations in other countries

Please contact Viva! (listed on p. 183) for a list of organisations in your country.

Resources

Vegan products list

For a list of food, drink, clothing, household/garden goods and animal care products that contain no animal ingredients, read the *Animal Free Shopper* by the Vegan Society, available from the Vegan Society or Viva! (see contact details on p.183.)

Non-leather shoes

You can buy non-leather shoes by mail order. Send for catalogues from:

Alchuringa, The Coach House, Derry Ormond Park, Lampeter, Dyfed SA48 8PA, UK.

Ethical Wares, 84 Clyde Way, Rise Park, Romford, Essex RM1 4UT, UK.

Heartland Products, Box 218, Dakota City, Iowa IA 50529, USA.

Moko, Severn House, 66 Spring Gardens, Shrewsbury, Shrops SY1 2TE, UK.

Vegan Wares, 78 Smith Street, Collingwood 3066, Australia.

Vegetarian Shoes, 12 Gardner Street, Brighton BN1 1UP, UK.

Vegetarian pets
The following companies sell veggie pet food by mail order. Send for details from:

Happidog (sells veggie dried dog food by mail order and cans in the shops), Bridgend Factory, Brownhill Lane, Longton, Preston, Lancs PR4 4S, UK.

Katz go Vegan, Box 161, The Vegan Society, Donald Watson House, St Leonards on Sea, E Sussex TN37 7AA, UK.

Natural Dog Food Co (dog food cereal), Audley Street, Mossley, Lancs 0L5 9HS, UK.

Pet shops also sell Wafcol dog food:
Wafcol, The Nutrition Bakery Haigh Avenue, Stockport, Cheshire SK4 1NU, UK.

Further Reading

If you have difficulty getting hold of these books, contact Viva! for their worldwide mail-order book catalogue, *Books for Life*. It contains books in all the following categories.

Vegetarian/vegan issues
Beyond Beef, Jeremy Rifkin, Plume, 1993
A Far Cry From Noah, Peter Stevenson, Green Print, 1994
Food For a Future, Jon Wynne-Tyson, Centaur Press, 1985
The New Why You Don't Need Meat, Peter Cox, Bloomsbury, 1994
The Silent Ark, (an exposé of meat, the global killer), Juliet Gellatley with Tony Wardle, Thorsons, 1996
Today's Poultry Industry, FAWN, 1995

Animal rights
Animal Liberation, Peter Singer, Thorsons, 1991
Animal Rights, Mark Gold, Jon Carpenter Publishing, 1995

The Dreaded Comparison, Marjorie Spiegel, Heretic Books, 1988

The Extended Circle, Jon Wynne-Tyson, Centaur Press, 1990

Roar! Animal Rights Handbook for Kids, Peter Hoggarth, Bloomsbury, 1996

Save the Animals — 101 Easy Things You Can Do, Ingrid Newkirk, Angus & Robertson, 1991

When Elephants Weep: The Emotional Lives of Animals, Jeffrey Masson and Susan McCarthy, Vintage, 1996

The Young Person's Action Guide to Animal Rights, Barbara James, Virago Press, 1992

Environmental issues

50 Simple Things Kids Can Do to Save The Earth, Earth Works Group

Causing a Stink! The Eco Warrior's Handbook, Caroline Clayton, Bloomsbury, 1996

The Last Green Book On Earth, Judy Allen and Martin Brown, Red Fox, 1994

The Young Green Consumer Guide, John Elkington and Julia Hailes, Gollancz, 1990

The Young Person's Guide to Saving The Planet, Debbie Silver and Bernadette Vallely, Virago Press, 1990

Nutrition/health

Eat Right, Live Longer, Dr Neal Barnard, PCRM, 1996

Peter Cox's Guide to Vegetarian Living, Bloomsbury, 1995

The Plants We Need to Eat, Jeanette Ewin, Thorsons, 1997

Stories/poems with a veggie theme

Anything Within Reason, Jon Wynne-Tyson, Centaur Press, 1994

The Chicken Gave It To Me, Anne Fine, Mammoth, 1996
Sealskin Trousers and Other Stories, Jon Wynne–Tyson, Centaur Press, 1994
Talking Turkeys, poems by Benjamin Zephaniah, Puffin Books, 1995
Victor the Vegetarian, Radha Vignola, AVIVA, 1996

Vegan recipes/food
The Absolutely Animal-Free Cookbook, Wendy Turner, Book Guild, 1997
Cooking with PETA, PETA, 1997
The L-Plate Vegan, Viva!, 1997
Green Gastronomy, Colin Spencer, Bloomsbury, 1996
The Single Vegan, Leah Leneman, Thorsons, 1989
Vegan Feasts, Rose Elliot, Thorsons, 1997

Vegetarian recipes/food
30 Minute Vegetarian Italian/Turkish/Thai/Indian/Mexican Cookbooks, Thorsons, 1997–1998
Classic 1000 Vegetarian Recipes, Carolyn Humphries, Foulsham, 1997
The L-Plate Vegetarian, Viva!, 1998
The New Student's Veggie Cookbook, Carolyn Humphries, Foulsham, 1997
Rose Elliot's Vegetarian Meals in Minutes, HarperCollins, 1998
Rose Elliot's Supreme Vegetarian Cookery, Thorsons, 1995

Further Reading – USA
All books are available from PETA (see p. 184)
A Teen's Guide to Going Vegetarian, Judy Krizmanic, Viking Children's Press, 1994

Diet for a New America, John Robbins, Stillpoint Publishing, 1987

Food for Life: How the New Four Food Groups Can Save Your Life, Neal Barnard, Harmony Books, 1993

Generation React: Activism for Beginners, Danny Seo, Ballantine, 1997

Further Reading – Australia

New Voices for the Animals, Animal Liberation SA, 1995 (see p. 187)

If you don't want these little piggies to go to market...

Join *Viva!*

Why *Viva!*?

Every year in Britain, more than 700 million animals face the barbarity of slaughter - many fully conscious. Most spend their short lives in confinement, pain and misery.

Every year the earth staggers closer to environmental disaster. Whether polluted water or torched forests; eroded topsoil or spreading deserts - livestock production is at the heart of the problem. Meanwhile, the oceans are dying from the constant rape of overfishing.

Every year, millions of people in the developing world die from hunger - alongside fields of fodder destined for the West's livestock.

Every year, proof increases that vegetarians are healthier than meat eaters. Overnight, with the simple decision to stop eating meat and fish, you cease to play a part in this insanity.

Saving Animals

Viva! is the only vegetarian and vegan charity in the UK dedicated to campaigning for farm animals. With regular hard-hitting campaigns, *Viva!* saves lives.

Get SCOFFin'!

SCOFF! is *Viva!*'s *Schools' Campaign Opposed to Factory Farming*. For a free pack with poster, leaflets and petition on how to help end cruelty to animals - send your name and address to *Viva!* (mark your envelope SCOFF!).

Going Veggie

And if you're a learner veggie, *Viva!* is here to help. Contact us for a free *Going Veggie* pack. For guides on what foods are easily available, buy the *L-Plate Vegetarian* or *L-Plate Vegan* (£1 each, including p&p).

Join Viva!

To join the best group in the cosmos (probably!), just send *Viva!* a cheque (payable to *Viva!*) for £4.99 (if under 18) or for £12 (if 18 or over) with your name, address and age. You'll receive special earth-savin', animal-liberatin' stickers, poster, leaflets and four issues of your own mini-mag *Vivactive!*. *Join Viva! and Join the Fight for Life!*

**Viva!, 12 Queen Square, Brighton BN1 3FD, UK   Tel: 01273 777688
E-mail: info@viva.org.uk Web Site: www.viva.org.uk**

Registered charity 1037486